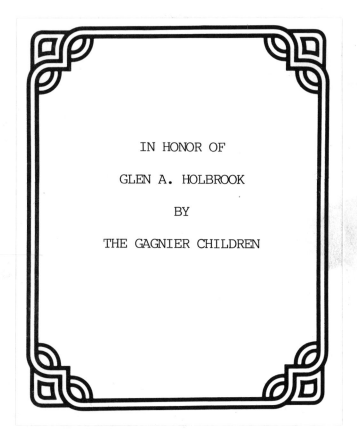

IN HONOR OF

GLEN A. HOLBROOK

BY

THE GAGNIER CHILDREN

PHEASANT HUNTER'S
HARVEST

Books by Steve Grooms

MODERN PHEASANT HUNTING

PHEASANT HUNTER'S HARVEST

PHEASANT HUNTER'S HARVEST

Steve Grooms

•———————•

Illustrated by Robert Halladay

LYONS & BURFORD, PUBLISHERS

Portions of this book have appeared—sometimes in different form—in *Shooting Sportsman, Fins and Feathers, Pheasants Forever, Wing & Shot,* and *Gun Dog.*

PRINTED IN THE UNITED STATES OF
AMERICA
10 9 8 7 6 5 4 3 2 1

Designed by Liz Driesbach

LIBRARY OF CONGRESS CATALOGING-
IN-PUBLICATION DATA

Grooms, Steve.
    Pheasant hunter's harvest / Steve Grooms;
illustrated by Robert Halladay.
        p.   cm.
    ISBN 1-55821-089-X (cloth) : $18.95
    1. Pheasant shooting. 2. Pheasant shooting—United States.
I. Title.
SK325.P5G73 1990
799.2'48617—dc20   90-42143
                                              CIP

This book is for my father,

GEORGE GROOMS,

who got me started in pheasant hunting

as well as in life;

and to

KATHE,

who sustains me in all ways

CONTENTS

ACKNOWLEDGMENTS

—•———————————•—

Although this is a very personal book, I had a great deal of help. Information, assistance, and moral support came from John Barsness, Al Beitz, Al Berner, Steve Bodio and the late Betsy Huntington, John Cardarelli, Jet Collins, Tom Davis, Larry Duke, Bill Gallea, Kathe Grooms, Jerry Hoffnagle, Tom Huggler, Jay Johnson, Gary and Nancy Johnson, Jim Layton, Jim Marti, Don Nelson, Steve Nelson, Michael Pearce, Rick Peifer, Hugh Price, Pat Redig, Tony Romano, John Scharf, Kenneth Solomon, John Wilson, Jim Wooley, and "Pam" at the Madison County Courthouse in Winterset, Iowa. Any errors in this book appear in spite of the good efforts of those people.

By rights, I should express my debt to several hunting dogs. I'll single out just two. Most of what I know about pheasants was taught me by Brandy. In effect, she wrote my first pheasant hunting book; I was just the amanuensis. Now Spook is adding his own elegant additions and corrections to those early lessons.

I'd like, also, to thank artist Robert Halladay for his wonderfully attractive contributions to the book. Kathe and I owe the pleasure of his friendship to pheasants, and pheasants continue to give us excuses to enjoy his company.

To all of you, my heartfelt thanks.

INTRODUCTION
Having the Fire

●——————————●

You have heard the benign cliché (often proposed in a schematic step-by-step form in hunter's education courses) that we progress through various stages in our hunting from rabid consumer to a sort of Schweitzerian reverence-for-life in which we no longer care about the "bag." Apart from the fact that humans aren't that simple, I fear that the average American hunter rarely evolves that far.

Pheasant Hunter's Harvest is a book about hunting pheasants, and you can learn more about pheasants, bird dogs, and American pheasant hunters from it than from any other book I have ever read. Steve Grooms's good-natured attacks on conventional wisdom in "The Bird" are worth the price of admission all by themselves. But it is even more a sort of *Pilgrim's Progress*, a living document of one passionate and sensitive hunter's life, of what the hunter's life is in our time.

Steve Grooms is not an Outdoor Writer—whatever that animal might be—but a writer: a person who is out there living his life with all his senses and his brain and his soul, then coming back to set down what he has seen and heard and smelled and tasted and felt and thought and learned, putting it down in the best words he can find, so that we, the readers, can feel and think and learn ourselves.

Yes, there's a life—and lives—between these covers. There are portraits of men and women and dogs as vivid as any novelist's, vistas as big as the open skies over the Dakotas and as limited as those seen when you're knee-deep in a midwestern cattail marsh. Perhaps above all, *Harvest* is a self-portrait, the life of a gung-ho hunter who is not afraid to admit that he wants to possess the bird he loves and yet has never seen it apart from the land and people that he loves as well.

Oh, yes, land. And time passing. Steve Grooms knows, and accepts that we and our dogs and our birds all die, and he neither ignores the fact nor covers it with cheap sentimentality. What he will not accept is the death of the land by our greedy, collective hand. Read "Prairie Rattler," his portrait of Jim Marti, the ornery and driven master breeder of English setters who lives in North Dakota and does more for conservation in a month than you or I are likely to do in a lifetime.

You picked up this book because you care a little about birds and dogs and, I hope, the land. Let Steve Grooms show you, remind you, about why you do.

As he says of Jim Marti: he has the fire.

—STEVE BODIO
Magdalena, NM, 1990

THE CAST

———•———————•———

In these pages you will frequently meet the people and dogs I have most often hunted with. I would like to introduce them now.

"Kathe" is my wife. Though not a hunter when we met, Kathe quickly learned to love upland hunting. She often prefers to go her own way, choosing her own pace and direction. Two energetic dogs live in our St. Paul home because one dog cannot hunt with both of us at once. Since Kathe is right-handed with a dominant left eye, she gets a cattywampus view of her barrels. She compensates by squinting ("like Popeye," she says), and has a double on ruffed grouse to her credit. Kathe's warm smile is a great asset when we stand at some stranger's door asking him to trust us to carry guns on his land. Above all, Kathe is a plucky, good-hearted, loving companion.

"Bill" is Bill Gallea, my most frequent hunting partner though he lives much farther from us than we wish he did. Bill is a family physician in a small town along the shores of Lake Superior, near Canada. He is a rarity: a highly intelligent and compassionate man with an active outdoor life. Many years ago, Bill introduced us to the delights of grouse hunting. I reciprocated by introducing him to pheasants, the bird of my youth. Bill and I have spent hundreds of hours in enthusiastic conversation in various vehicles as we drove to distant pheasant fields. Many of the major decisions of our lives were made in those vehicles—decisions to marry, to buy homes, to have children, to bring dogs into our lives. The decisions have proven to be as good as the trips.

"Jerry" is Jerry Hoffnagle, another close friend who lives too far away. Jerry has a quirky, analytical mind and an eye that misses nothing. He writes strange letters in which bon mots of sociological observation bob merrily in a sea of typos. Jerry shared with us the finest pheasant hunting we are ever likely to know. His encouragement made it possible for me to write both my first book and this one. Thanks to Jerry, I have been able to see pheasant hunting again through the eyes of an enthusiastic beginner.

And myself? I was raised in central Iowa in a time when pheasants were common and hunting them almost easy. I fell in love with pheasants then and have pursued them with more ardor than sense for more than three decades. Because I live in the land of the wind chill factor where pheasants are scarce, I do much of my hunting on expeditions to regions more blessed with birds. Pheasant hunting isn't something I enjoy; it is my grand passion.

Those are the people. These are the dogs.

"Brandy" is the dominant character in these pages, for it was she who taught me to hunt. A springer spaniel, Brandy was my first hunting dog. She hunted with swashbuckling abandon through thirteen seasons. There was no quit in Brandy. She and I were foolishly young together and went on to hunt together long enough to become perfect partners, two bodies working from one mind. I understand now that I'll never stop missing her.

"Pogo" was with me for two years before moving to another family when I got Spook. Pogo loved to hunt, but only one day at a stretch. My crash-and-burn five-day safaris were, in Pogo's eyes, far too much of a good thing. Pogo now lives in South Dakota with a man who takes her out frequently but only for an hour or two. Pogo thinks she was transferred to Heaven and wouldn't come back to me under any circumstances.

"Spook" is my partner these days, a classy young English setter who smiles as he hunts. Like Brandy, Spook is deeply devoted to his people and mad about birds. Unlike Brandy, Spook has the manners of a gentleman. In him the desire to get a bird is balanced with a sense of honor about the proper and improper ways of accomplishing that. With legs, nose, brains, and style, Spook has it all. Like a few great dancers or athletes, he is incapable of looking anything but graceful and handsome at every moment.

"Pukka" was Kathe's first hunting dog. A butter-yellow Labrador, Pukka had a body builder's physique and a curiously wired-tight personality. I always thought of her as a male. Pukka was happy only when in motion. When we attempted to fondle her, Pukka became agitated and sought something to retrieve. Pukka was a fey spirit who adored us deeply without ever learning how to show it. She was with us for only three years before a car struck her. Pukka died as she had lived, in full flight.

"Brinka" then became Kathe's partner. Another yellow Lab, Brinka had the sweetest disposition I've seen in a dog. Alas, Brinka was given every attribute of a great pheasant dog except sound hips, so her career with us was cut tragically short. She spent her final years as someone's fat house pet. But if Brinka dreamt in her post-hunting years, I know the color and shape of those dreams, and they were damn good.

"Tessie," a freckled imp of a springer who shares some of

Brandy's bloodlines, is Kathe's dog these days. Some hunters would criticize Tessie's limited range. Not Kathe, who spent years watching Brandy flushing birds at such distances we couldn't identify their sex and sometimes not their species. Tess is pretty and knows it. I often envy her because Tessie has never for a moment doubted the absolute perfection of her body and her every act. Tessie adores strutting smugly with something precious in her mouth, which may be why she retrieves so well.

Those are the hunters, human and canine, whose exploits make up this book. All are or were highly imperfect hunters. All, that is, except Spook, who might be perfect although he sometimes practices his perfection somewhat farther from his master than he might. All are, or were, beloved field companions.

INTROIT

—•— 1 —•—

I owe a great deal to pheasants.

The earliest debt is my first definite recollection of my father. He left our family to help fight a war when I was a toddler with a muzzy awareness of my surroundings. But he returned home for a brief leave when I was three, and I remember that. We went pheasant hunting, Dad and I, just the two of us. He recalls the experience somewhat ruefully. Spotting a rooster in a ditch, Dad jammed on the brakes of the 1940 Oldsmobile, pitching me headfirst into the windshield. But what I remember was sharing with my father a mission that crackled with tension and significance. We were hunting *pheasants!*

Pheasants caused me to enter the world of hunting dogs. That was some time ago, and several dogs have come and gone since. Kathe and I have a number of fragrant and sun-bleached old collars that we can't throw away because the memories are vibrantly alive though the collar owner is not. I was originally motivated to buy a hunting dog by simple concupiscence: I wanted to bag more birds. I now see that to have lived without dogs would have been a deprivation comparable to not having had children.

In a similar way, my discovery of prairie was due to pheasants. Kathe and I never would have made a long westward drive without the promise of pheasants to lure us. When I first beheld the wind-whipped Missouri Breaks I realized I had always carried in my heart a specific yearning to be in this place. That was *deja vu* with a twist: not feeling I had known this place before but feeling I had always been meant to know it.

I owe that to pheasants, that and so much more. I haven't yet mentioned all the friends and eccentric characters we've met in pheasant country. Or candlelight evenings that featured pheasants, story-telling, and glasses of dark red wine. Or the many startling discoveries of love and beauty in places I had not expected them. My life has been immeasurably enriched by pheasants.

A hunter sallies forth in pursuit of pheasants and sometimes finds them and sometimes does not. At the time, he thinks the finding is what matters. Later he looks back over it all and sees that the magic of the sport consists of all the other things he found while trying to find pheasants. They are the true pheasant hunter's harvest.

The chapters that follow represent my best effort to share one man's experience of a lifetime of hunting pheasants. I want to try to describe the whole experience, including the moments of unanticipated discovery that usually get left out of hunting stories.

If the words come right, readers will know this wonderful gamebird as I have known him. Knowing him so, they cannot fail to respect and love him. For it is his bird—this cocky, subtle, courageous, and extravagantly beautiful bird—that makes pheasant hunting the intoxicating, frustrating, and altogether wonderful sport that it is.

Not long ago, while riding in a car bumping along a two-track Dakota prairie road, I announced I had the "fire in the belly" problem. I was grossly misunderstood, as three hunters frantically cranked down windows to let in fresh air. Actually, I was referring to a Minnesota politician's curiously candid confession several years ago that he lacked the inexhaustible reservoirs of raw ambition needed to mount a campaign for the Presidency.

Older hunters know what it is to feel the fire in the belly smolder and dwindle. Once there was nothing within the bounds of legal conduct I would not do to shoot a rooster. Now there are many things I will not do because I have learned how they feel. Once I considered I'd failed if I quit hunting before limiting out. I no longer measure the quality of my hunts by body count.

What seems puzzling is how long it took to get to this point. I remain convinced that maturity doesn't evolve out of pureness of spirit, nor does it automatically occur at a certain age. Maturity, if that's what it is, depends in large measure upon hunting successfully so often that one no longer feels the need to prove anything.

These thoughts first suggested themselves to me when I began driving by cocks standing in ditches, birds that were perfectly legal and get-at-able. I haven't intentionally "road hunted" for thirty years, but most of my life I have hungered for roosters too keenly to drive past those prominently displayed in roadsides. Now I grin and honk to shoo them out of the sight of serious road hunters (if that isn't a self-contradictory phrase).

When I began bypassing roadside roosters, the question naturally asserted itself: "Hey, you just drove by a *pheasant!* If you aren't out here for pheasants, what *are* you hunting for?" In time, the answers came. I hunt for beauty, for challenge, for friendship, for the joy of working with a dog, for the drama of the encounter, and for the sense of accomplishment that follows from doing it right. At a slightly deeper level, I hunt to get in touch with an atavistic self that takes pure animal delight in the contest between hunter and hunted. In pheasant hunting I find my senses sharpened, my blood racing, and my whole being focused on what I am doing. I kill in order to have lived.

Well, fine.

There is nothing original in these perceptions, though each of us comes to them on our own. In fact, it is one of life's sly jokes that all the great personal truths we discover turn out to be clichés. Wisdom, when we have bled and suffered and sinned our way to it, turns out to be something we have read in a fortune cookie. The hazard of immaturity is that we debase ourselves and the sport in order to succeed. The hazard of maturity is that we become stultifying bores, congratulating ourselves endlessly for having triumphed over the fires of blood lust when, in fact, the process is natural and no great personal distinction.

I see another hazard. The minute a man decides it isn't really pheasants but something more spiritual he is hunting, it becomes easy to taper off. Pheasant hunting hurts. You walk for hours in places the human body wasn't meant to go. You bump into things, step on things, and fall into things that don't feel good. Often you do this in horrific weather. Pheasant hunting is no sport for mellow aesthetes. The trout angler can remove the fly, give his quarry a kiss, and send him finning home. But the hunter who shoots a rooster must smite him a terrible blow or face the nasty task of finishing the job by hand. Pheasant hunting is inherently aggressive and violent. If you aren't doing it totally, with a hot hammering heart, you aren't doing it at all.

And then a final hazard: the danger of thinking too much about something. I now imagine myself on the back step of some Iowa farmhouse, straining to explain my mission. The farmer, a genial freckled figure in stocking feet, holds his storm door open to hear me out. I stammer, "I was wondering if you'd let me and my dog work your fields. We're, uh, we're pheasant hunting. Sort of. Of course, what I'm actually seeking are some, ummm, epiphanies, though I suppose we'll have to shoot a few of your roosters to get them." The farmer sustains a frozen smile as he debates calling the constable to fetch this weirdo away in a coat with many buckles.

The irony is delicious. I now understand it is not "really" pheasants I am hunting, yet I must *really* hunt pheasants in order to earn those less corporeal experiences I treasure. Somehow, hunting was easier, maybe even morally cleaner, when I was dumb enough to think dead roosters were the object of the sport.

I've looked for years for a painting of pheasant hunting that got it right. So far, none has come very close. In the meantime, I carry the painting in my head, a commission that waits to be assigned when the right artist steps forward.

My painting has as its setting a November prairie landscape in the refulgent light of late afternoon. High above the prairie, a flock of sandhill cranes gyres in a thermal. The land itself has topographical complexity, reach, and majesty. Like so much prairie, it feels like a vast amphitheater designed to be the setting for some unimaginably important event.

In the foreground are two hunters. Rendering them will be the easiest and least important task for the painter. We see their backs only. Society and art are both so primitively evolved that artists never place women in hunting canvases. But I have hunted pheasants with the woman I love, so in my painting one of the hunters has ash blond hair swinging below her cap.

And a dog. Of course, a dog. If I followed my heart, there would be many dogs. Brandy would be there, and Brinka and Tess and Pukka and Pogo. They all have claims on my heart that cannot be denied. But having let in that many, how could

I say no to Pawnee, Rip, Archie, Ellie, and Rex? Acch! That's too many dogs, even for a limitless prairie, even for an intemperate dog lover like me.

So I settle for one dog. I see Spook in my painting, radiant steam wreathing his muzzle. He stands with an expression of high seriousness, as proud as an exclamation point, bedazzled by scent.

And now the impossible part, the bird. He is up, slashing air with blurry wings, not so much angry or alarmed as defiant. He is . . . but what can I say? You can see a wood duck or an elk, but you cannot see a flushing rooster. He is experienced, not seen. And even when the smell of gunpowder hangs in the air you cannot describe what it was you saw as you fired. Moments later, with the silky warm body in your hand, you cannot name for sure the color of his iridescent head. Like a dying dolphin, he alters colors as you watch.

That ideal painting will never make it to canvas. If it did, it would die in the process and be as disappointing as a taxidermist's stuffed grayling. The painting lives the only place it can, in my mind. Yet I go out each fall in pursuit of it.

ONE ON ONE

— • 2 • —

I learned to hunt pheasants in gangs. Like football, it was a group activity. The hunting parties of my youth ranged in size from six to a dozen men, if boys were counted as men; which they were, with much solemnity, and being counted a man was one compelling reason for a kid to hunt.

We needed all those bodies.

Consider where we hunted: cornfields, usually standing cornfields that spanned the horizons. In those pre-herbicide days our Iowa cornfields harbored a luxuriant understory of cockleburs, pigweed, foxtail, smartweed, and wild grasses. A 1950s cornfield was part of the natural world. It had ecological complexity, and wild things lived in it.

We had no dogs. I hiked many miles through six autumns in central Iowa without once seeing a hunting dog in the field. Dogs were considered an affectation of snooty East Coast hunters.

Under the circumstances, we hunted pheasants the only way we could. Frankly, we didn't know much about pheasant habits or pheasant cover. Yet we knew what worked. We got our pheasants by driving or surrounding them. We just needed a lot of human helpers.

Our tactics had a military aura. We marched in lines like parade ground soldiers. A boy stumbling with short legs over snarled rows of cornstalks kept learning he wasn't quite a man yet, but *"Keep in line!"* was the constant refrain from grownups. Our quarry could slip through gaps in a ragged line.

The simplest tactic was the straight-ahead drive with a long line of carefully spaced hunters. When we got fancy we'd position flankers slightly ahead on each side to contain pheasants trying to curl around the line. If we had to hunt a "clean" cornfield, one with few weeds, we anticipated wild-running pheasants. Then the party would split into equal numbers of drivers and blockers. The drivers rushed at the blockers in what military men call the "hammer and anvil" maneuver. When hammer met anvil there were sparks.

The shooting was as communal as the rest of the hunt. Any rooster visible above the corn was a fair target for one and all. My dad's shiny old Remington pump held six shots, and he commonly shot it dry in those apocalyptic moments when the trap was snapped shut on a pheasant flock and long-tailed birds filled the sky. We rarely knew who had downed a particular rooster, but that wasn't supposed to matter. The pile of birds was divvied up, anyway.

Yet on a November afternoon I still remember across the span of three decades, two cock birds erupted from the corn to vector in front of me like the targets in doubles trap. I dumped the right rooster, then saw the left bird crumple over my barrel at my second shot. That was my first double . . . or was until my friend Mike proudly popped the second cock in his game bag. His first shot and my second, perfectly synchronous, had made a single report. Such moments test the soul of a youth.

Mike was an errant shot. Vanity's voice thundered in my ear, "You *know* you got that bird, so claim the double!" Friendship and a fledgling code of fair play gently exhorted, "You've already got one rooster. Don't snatch Mike's only bird from him."

Years passed. I married Kathe. She and I learned a new style of pheasant hunting from Gary and Jan Crawford and their swampbusting Labradors, Pawnee and Rip. The Crawfords showed us that a party of four hunters and two dogs could shag roosters out of heavy cover more effectively than could the little armies I'd marched with as a kid.

Our small group could move, stop, and pivot with ease. When the cover changed size or direction we could adjust our drive without first needing to call a summit conference. Our tactics were scaled-down versions of those I'd been taught by my father. Four hunters could run drives and even block the ends of some confined strips of weeds. We couldn't sweep as many acres of cover as I had as a youth, so we compensated. We bypassed big but weedless fields in favor of compact spots choked with cover thick enough to tempt roosters to hold for a close flush.

I decided small-group hunting was pheasant hunting at its acme.

Soon Kathe and I had our own dogs. I hunted behind Brandy. Note the choice of words: I hunted *behind*, not with, my rocketing springer. The man was never born who could stay with Brandy on one of her frequent hell-for-leather dashes through the weeds. From dawn to dusk, Brandy hunted with the percussive energy of a ticker tape machine.

That created my either-or dilemma. Either I could stay in formation with my human partners. Or I could try to be somewhere near Brandy when she struck scent and went zooming off on another wild rooster chase. Rarely could I do both at once. For a while I experienced acute discomfort. I wanted to hunt with the politeness and discipline drilled into me as a youngster. But I also wanted results, and all the bird action was wherever Brandy was, which was usually fairly far away and getting farther by the second. I felt stupid staying in formation while she was gaily flushing cocks on the far side of the slough.

Willy nilly, I had been launched into hunting pheasants without human helpers.

Although necessity drove me to solo hunting, by the time Brandy mellowed enough to allow us to join groups again, my heart had forever turned against gang hunting. I was no longer my father's son. I no longer suffered the slightest twinges of guilt when I broke ranks to gallop after my dog. Going one-on-one with roosters had come to feel like the right and true way to hunt them.

There are practical reasons for hunting alone. In today's pheasant cover, with today's pheasant populations, the one-man, one-dog team enjoys advantages over parties cluttered with more people. The sloughs that held sixty pheasants when I was a kid might hold six now, with a pair of cocks among them. These days, hunting parties as small as three hunters might be out of proportion to bird numbers.

The solo hunter is free to work the best cover the landscape offers. That isn't always possible with groups, even small groups. The bird-wise solo hunter can sometimes hunt a whole day without setting foot outside the very choicest cover.

Of course, there are times when having another person or two around is helpful. With some small pieces of cover the smart approach is to ring the spot before approaching it. No matter how skillful a solo hunter might be, surrounding anything is a tall order. If the landscape offers something high— like a line of osage orange trees along a fence or a lofty patch of horseweeds—nineteen roosters out of twenty will blind-side the solo hunter, flushing from the back side of the obstruction. You hear them. You don't see them.

Brandy and I once spent an hour picking our way around the sloppy edge of a South Dakota marsh. In the whole swamp the only object higher than my eyes was a stand of phragmites. Brandy suddenly slammed into the phragmites. Because I was on the east side, the rooster (of course, of course!) went out the west side, sassing me mercilessly. I heard him. I didn't see him.

I once assumed a lone hunter could work narrow strips and isolated cover patches more efficiently than large fields. Often, the opposite is true. Educated roosters caught in narrow or patchy cover are keenly aware of their vulnerability and often flush when you are too far away to shoot. As a solo hunter I now love working monster blocks of cover, exactly the sort of place I used to consider impossible without human accomplices. As long as the cover isn't so thin birds refuse to sit for a flush, the solo hunter with a dog operates at no disadvantage in huge fields. Experience tells me a rooster in a large block of good cover is more cocksure than he'd be in a patch. He's less likely to panic when I am fifty yards away, more likely to try cute tricks in the weeds. Spook and I live for the moments when roosters try cute tricks.

Perhaps solo pheasant hunting sounds self-centered, just what you'd expect the Me Generation to do to the fine traditions of a gregarious sport. I disagree.

Bill and I hunted some South Dakota draws south of Pierre several years ago. When Bill's splendid young Lab, Ellie, got scent, we stopped to watch her work the trail out. Suddenly Brandy shot in, having picked up the scent farther back. She blew by Ellie as if she weren't there. Moments later the old springer was proudly retrieving the rooster Bill shot. Bill accepted that bird with a look of dismay. He'd had a special moment stolen from him just as I'd lost my first double. During hundreds of hours of backyard training, Bill dreamed of the day Ellie would trail, flush, and retrieve a cock for him. And now this.

"If it's all right with you," Bill said, "I'll head off on my own with Ellie. There are things we need to do that won't happen with a dog like Brandy nearby." When we met up later, Bill was beaming. Ellie had put it all together, giving him great shots on two pheasants that she retrieved to hand (having first jerked out their tails—pups will be pups!).

Indeed, dogs are why I love solo hunts as I do. There are still places in this tragically over-developed world where two or three dogs can slash boldly through cover without snarling up each other's program, yet they are rare. Spook, like Brandy before him, lives to hunt. I owe it to him to give him chances to hunt his best, where other dogs won't cramp his style.

We are a team. I've spent over thirty years learning the ways of pheasants. Hunting pheasants one-on-one in today's heavily pressured fields is a high challenge, yet one we occasionally meet with distinction. I know if I give him a fair chance, from time to time Spook will do something so beautiful and clever I'll be moved to awe.

Other people get in the way of that. Bringing other hunters into our hunts doesn't prevent us from bagging birds, but bagged birds are not the point of our hunts. The point of our pheasant hunting is to attempt something difficult and to do it well; to do it, if you will, with honor. Often a bird is just too good for us, which is as it should be. But when Spook and I prevail, we have done something right and we've done it without outside help.

All of this is not to criticize the good folks who enjoy the camaraderie of gang hunting. Group hunting works, it is ethical, and for many people it satisfies more than my lone wolf hunts. To each his own. I enjoy having friends nearby. Best of all are those hunts when I can look across a field to see a friend and a dog working together, and no hunt is complete unless companions gather at day's end to share experiences. At times it delights me to walk with an open gun behind Spook, letting a friend take the birds he conjures up.

Ultimately, the land and the bird and the dog form a holy triangle. From time to time it is my enormous privilege to enter that triangle. There is a purity and intensity about that simple relationship that breaks down when other people—even people I love—complicate it with their presence.

Some things are best done in groups. Some things are best done as couples. Some things, like talking to God or hunting pheasants, are best done alone.

OUR HERO

— • 3 • —

Confession, they say, is good for the soul. Here are some stories I lacked the courage to tell earlier.

I once held a teaching job that allowed me to sneak away for short afternoon hunts. My hunting vehicle was a fuschia 1958 Chevrolet, the most repulsive color of the ugliest car Detroit ever made. One day, feeling frisky, I took a quick hunt with our two young dogs, Pukka and Brandy. After a short drive north of town, I parked the Fuschia Bomb near a field that sometimes gave us a rooster or two.

Neither dog had been trained to hunt under control and neither, I assure you, did. Just two years old and full of the pazizzies, Brandy and Pukka whizzed around me like electrons circulating a nucleus. As I'd feared, each dog spurred the other to fresh heights of reckless idiocy.

The pups and I careened westward, throwing mud, panting, and crashing into each other. There was a patch of willows that once had held a grouse, so we rammed through it. From behind me, a woodcock helicoptered drunkenly into the sky. I recovered my wits in time to drop it. A woodcock! That was about the last thing I'd expected.

We then turned our attention back to thick weeds and pheasants. Brandy got birdy in a patch of high slough grass. The bird ran. The pups and I thundered in pursuit for perhaps forty yards before flushing—to my utter amazement—a ruffed grouse. He was the only grouse I've ever found in hip-high grass and the only grouse that ever ran before my dogs through weeds like an educated rooster.

We next came to an irrigation ditch overgrown with brome and reed canary grass. When Pukka began nosing intently in the weeds, I didn't know what to expect. Perhaps a peacock. It was that kind of day. But it was a rooster, a big old guy, and he was soon in my game bag beside the grouse and woodcock.

Hey, I thought, this experiment of hunting with two untrained dogs was working out pretty well. We weren't winning any style points, but the results were nice. One more rooster would fill my Minnesota limit, with a bonus grouse and woodcock. I only regretted that I'd taken three birds of different species with three shots and didn't have an eyewitness to do my boasting for me.

For the next hour the pups and I buzzsawed through cover without result. When we approached a small patch of weeds in a spot of low ground in a cornfield, both dogs got hot. A movement caught my eye. A rooster, his head and tail clamped low, was legging it away from us down a row in the corn. He'd soon be out of range.

I ran at him, hollering. I don't know what other people say at such times, but I roared, *"You!* Hey *you!"* The pheasant didn't linger to hear what I might say next. I kept running and howling like a waiter chasing a diner trying to skip the check. Finally he flushed, a smallish rooster with a short tail. I put on the brakes and hurled a load of sixes at him. My first shot missed (there went the string of perfect shooting) and the second shot was only marginally better. The pheasant fluttered down in a strip of weeds that eventually connected with the irrigation ditch far to the north of us.

Brandy and Pukka raced each other to the fallen bird. Several moments of frantic searching didn't turn him up. I ran to assist them because I knew my hit was poor. Brandy rammed ahead of me, snuffling madly in the weeds. Pukka horned in ahead of her. Brandy leap-frogged Pukka. I ran in front of Brandy.

Then all three of us took off like greyhounds after a tin bunny. I couldn't tell which dog had the hottest scent. God, the dogs looked hot! I gritted my teeth, held my shotgun like a relay baton, and kicked out my legs with wild abandon. We sprinted all the way down the strip—over a hundred yards—to the irrigation ditch.

Only when we reached the ditch did I begin to suspect neither dog had been working scent. "Where's the bird?" I demanded of Brandy. Brandy looked blankly from me to Pukka and back to me. "Geez, it beats me! I thought *she* had the scent." Pukka frowned quizzically. "*Me,* oh gosh no! I was just keeping ahead of the bearded guy. I thought *he* knew where it went!"

We three puffed and stared daggers at each other for several minutes, then hiked back to where the bird fell. We kicked around that area for several minutes without finding anything more exciting than a few body feathers. I gave up and headed off hunting again. My wonderful little hunt was falling apart on me.

This was a difficult period of my life, a time when the voice of my interior monologue had assumed the supercilious singsong tone of a popular television football commentator. Now that man's voice was in my head, where I couldn't tune it out, analyzing my shooting in terms that made me want to crawl into a hole.

On top of everything else, Pukka had gone missing. I yelled for her with mounting anger. She'd never misbehaved this badly before. I hollered until I was hoarse. "Pukka! You *COME!*" No response. "Hey, Pukka, how'd you like a nice big *shock collar* for Christmas? I could put a new spark in your life, Pooks!"

Minutes later something brushed my knee. I turned to find the missing Labrador walking on heel behind me with a tailless but lively rooster in her mouth. She'd probably been there all along. Still, I was furious with her the way I get with Kathe when she hides my socks by putting them in my socks drawer. I broke the bird's neck and popped him in my bag. We hunted the ditch back to the car, a walk of almost an hour. I began feeling lucky again. Maybe there would be another grouse in the weeds. Or a capercaile. It was that kind of day.

Back at the car I produced a camera and lined up my birds to immortalize the unusual mixed bag. Whoops! Where is that second rooster? There was the big fellow, there was the grouse and, okay, the woodcock . . . but the little no-tail rooster was AWOL. I groped inside my game bag. Aargh! There was a hole in one corner, just big enough.

He had to be somewhere. I set off walking on our back trail, bent at the waist like an old man, studying the ground for my lost bird. The voice in my head was describing my conduct with acidic sarcasm. The pups, grumbling protests, were put on heel so they could find him with their keen noses. With luck, he'd be close to the car.

It seemed our luck had been used up. I backtracked all the way to where I'd shot the pheasant. No bird. Oh well, there was a little shooting light left. We set off hunting again. No telling what might happen.

Brandy was zooming around in high spirits, relieved to be free of her detested *Heel* command. But where was that damned Labrador? Pukka was nowhere in sight. I bellowed her name and blew my whistle (ignoring the fact she hadn't been trained to come to it). She wouldn't come in. As I stomped along, my face violet with rage, I tried to invent a punishment suitably awful for Pukka if she returned. I howled threats at the weeds, hoping the wicked Labrador could hear. "Hey, Pukka, some people in this world *eat* dogs! Wouldn't you look fancy in a roasting pan with an apple in your mouth?"

Then something brushed my leg. There was Pukka, politely on heel, with the little no-tail rooster in her mouth. Though I had killed him twice already, his head was up. The voice in my head was so full of contempt for me he was spitting all over his mike.

As the long shadows of evening melded with the anonymous gloom of nightfall, I drove the Fuschia Bomb home. Two muddy pups snored happily in the back seat. The best thing about the hunt, I concluded, was there had been no eyewitnesses.

The first time Brandy bayed like a bloodhound I almost wet my pants with fear. It was a horrible, desperate sound.

We were in an aspen grouse woods north of town. Typically, I couldn't see Brandy, whose theory of grouse hunting was to make all the birds fly away before I could get close enough to do it myself. Then I heard a sound—*Awrooo! Awrooo!*—like the hound of the Baskervilles. "My God," I thought, "Brandy's in trouble! She caught her collar on something and she's *hanging!*" I dropped my gun and ran recklessly through the timber to save her.

Then a big donkey-eared snowshoe hare loped by. Close behind was Brandy, very much alive, baying lustily. *Awrooo! Awrooo!* I could still hear her howling in the distance while I searched for my gun. Brandy returned about the time I found it, some fifty minutes later.

After that, I recognized that awful noise when I heard it. But the whole business was a mystery. Brandy hunted all sorts of birds without baying. She chased running roosters without giving tongue. What about rabbits caused her to bawl like a bluetick?

The answer came one afternoon when we were working a railroad track in central Iowa. Brandy bounced a rooster out of some horseweeds. When I brought the gun up on him I could see several Herefords in the background. Shooting cows is one sure way to sour hunter-farmer relations, so I kept swinging with the bird until he had an open sky behind him. Then I carefully shot him in the last joint of his left wing.

I knew we were looking for a strong running cripple. Brandy burrowed in the weeds along the track, then darted off across a fall-plowed field. I followed, teetering from clod to clod. The trail led to a grassy fenceline. As so many Iowa fences do, this one had hog wire strung at ground level. Hog wire is a metal mesh that contains pigs better than naked strands of barbed wire.

I saw the rooster running just ahead of us. Brandy moved in to grab him. As she opened her mouth, the bird scooted through a square in the hog wire. Brandy was too big to follow. Now the rooster was running with Brandy matching him stride for stride on the wrong side of the wire.

Awrooo! Awrooo! Brandy bayed agonies from the depths of her soul.

A light went on in my head. I saw that Brandy bayed from frustration, specifically the frustration of seeing something she wanted but could not catch. That category included all rabbits and now this rooster.

I caught up with Brandy. Grabbing her collar and the skin over her butt, I dumped her over the fence.

She moved in on the rooster.

He popped through a square back to my side.

Awrooo! Awrooo!

Let me insert a confession here. I've long been squeamish

about handling lively roosters, the result of coming out second best in a little *mano-a-mano* fracas with a sharp-spurred cock when I was a kid. I wanted Brandy to deal with this guy.

I scaled the fence and threw Brandy back on the side with the bird. She moved in on him. The rooster squirted through the hog wire again, leaving Brandy separated from him by inches. So close, but so far.

Awrooo! Awrooo!

Even a dull fellow gets the point after enough repetitions. Each time I pitched Brandy over the fence, the rooster would come back to my side. We could do this all afternoon.

So I charged the bird while Brandy brayed lugubriously on the wrong side of the wire. From a running start I launched myself in a flying tackle, my body laid out flat on the air like a javelin. When I crashed back to earth the rooster was somewhere else, but he was newly impressed with me as a threat. He zipped through the hog wire, where Brandy nailed him.

Back at the car, I met up with Kathe, who had taken Pukka the other direction on the tracks.

"Oho, success! No secrets now—how'd you get him?"

"Well, ummm, there were these cows, and . . . Geez, it's hard to explain. You hadda been there."

Spook and I never knew the rooster was there until he flushed from behind my right shoulder and slanted to the east, going quick and low. I spun and shot. The bird dropped, though I wasn't confident he was down for keeps. Since Spook didn't retrieve, I ran toward where I'd marked the bird down. I soon found myself on the west bank of an irrigation canal. On the east bank I could see the tail feathers of my rooster pointed straight at the sky.

Spook was confused. He hadn't seen or smelled anything so he wondered why I'd fired my gun. "I don't suppose you want to swim over there and bring him back, do you?" I asked. That is what is known as a rhetorical question. Spook cocked an ear and looked earnest.

I examined the canal, a rather steep-sided thing. At its bottom, black water flowed smoothly and opaquely along. I looked for stones or a log or a beaver dam or anything to help me cross. Nothing. Minnesota creeks are cold in mid-November, and this was a see-your-breath sort of day. A guy doesn't want to walk in water over his boots then. The water was only about seven feet across, maybe a tad more. I no longer can leap seven feet while wearing a hunting coat full of shells. I never could.

I held my gun on the rooster for a moment and considered touching off an anchoring shot. But he was head down, tail up, going nowhere.

Spook and I hiked upstream to find a crossing spot. The canal was maddeningly uniform. Seven feet. I couldn't believe there were no beavers on this waterway. Seven feet. We went farther. Seven feet. Dammit, isn't that just like a beaver . . . always around when you don't want them and never there when you do? We finally drew uncomfortably near a farm. That's a crummy way to meet farmers—barging in unannounced from the back side of the place, dirty and puffing, gun in hand.

I looked at the canal. Seven feet. It was time to quit dithering around and make a manly commitment. I unloaded my SKB and chucked it across the canal into some reed canary grass. "There!" I told Spook with satisfaction. "We've made up our minds, haven't we? *We cross here!*" If he'd been more educated I could have made some knowing comments about crossing Rubicons.

I knew I wouldn't make it if I launched my leap from dry ground on the near side. Too far. So I planned to dash down the slope of the canal and plant my right boot just a short distance into the water. Then by punching it hard I could come down on my left boot in shallow water just inches from the far side of the canal.

These things always seem to take place in slow motion. The lumbering run down the slope went as well as I could expect. The planting of the right foot, however, was most disappointing. Rather than jumping from three or four inches of water, as I'd hoped, my boot splooshed down in two feet of water. I knew the leap was doomed before it was started, but now was committed as much by momentum as the shotgun on the far side.

The arc of my trajectory carried me high over the canal, then decayed. I seemed to hang over black water for eternity before bellywhopping squarely in the middle of the canal. Aftershocks sent creek water sloshing out on both banks. *My,* that water was brisk! I dog-paddled furiously until I could seize some grass on the far side and haul myself out. I was drenched in ice water from the ears on down.

Spook's eyes were like saucers. He couldn't believe what he'd seen.

The rooster? Oh, he was gone long before I squished back to where he'd landed.

THIS BIRD

———— • 4 • ————

Basically, we're talking about a fancy chicken.

Pheasants are gallinaceous birds, meaning they are members of the chicken clan. Galliformes are plump, ground-dwelling birds that scratch for food. Pheasants are distinguished from other galliformes by the glorious plumage, the leg spurs, and the showy tail of the males.

Early ancestors of pheasants were five feet tall. I, for one, am glad they aren't still around. Fossil remains of birds recognizable as pheasants have been dated to the Miocene era. The Chinese were stitching recognizable golden and silver pheasants in tapestries thirty-five centuries ago. The oldest written record of pheasants comes from the Greek dramatist, Aeschylus, writing in the fifth century B.C.

An adult fall rooster is "almost three"—almost three feet long, almost three pounds. Cocks of the year are a few ounces lighter and inches shorter. Hens are "about two"—about two pounds in weight and just under two feet long. There are reports, discounted by some authorities, of monster ringnecks tipping the scales at five pounds.

Why is the rooster as resplendent as a plumed cavalier from the court of Louis the XV? In a word: sex. In four words: because he can't sing.

The bird world can be roughly divided between good lookers and good singers. Birds either look good or sound good, rarely both. Male songbirds attract mates by filling the air with skeins of dulcet notes. Many songbirds are drab little fellows living inconspicuously in heavy timber. If songbirds couldn't sing, they'd never be able to swing a date at mating time.

The mating game is different for birds of the open plains, birds like pheasants. Since they can't sing, they dance or strike sexy poses. To call the rooster a wretched singer is to flatter him. His self-important squawk is as sweet to the ear as chalk skritching on a blackboard. Never mind. When you look *that* good, you need not worry how you sound.

One can paint the demure hen with only three little tubes of paint. Buff, black, and cream will do for Mrs. Ringneck. She was designed to be nearly invisible when hunkered in dry grass over her eggs.

To render her flamboyant beau, a painter needs a palette large enough to hold at least thirteen daubs of paint: tan, olive, purple, copper, black, gray, powder blue, brown, russet, white, crimson, iridescent green and iridescent indigo. He is a flashy dresser, as subtle as a Mardi Gras celebrant.

Taxidermists, photographers, and wildlife artists have collaborated to confuse each other and everyone else about what a pheasant looks like. Roosters are camera-shy in fall. Virtually all closeup photos of roosters on the ground are taken in spring. Then a cock trying to impress his ladies will puff up like a blowfish and stare contemptuously at a photographer grinding film through his motor drive. Consequently, most closeup photos of roosters show prominent ear tufts (pinnae) and a wattle that is both enlarged and engorged—characteristics of spring roosters. The pinnae of fall roosters are barely visible, if at all, and their wattles are shriveled.

Though taxidermists know that, they also know those protruding pinnae add drama to a mount. While they can't make a fall rooster's wattle as prominent as it is in spring, little tufts of cotton under the pinnae yield a mount with prominent feathery horns.

Enter the painter. Working with mounted birds as models, the painter produces flying roosters with protruding pinnae, smoothly cupped wings, and perfectly symmetrical tails. Painters often show roosters rising at sensationally steep angles with their necks bent like rattlesnakes about to strike. A painter reaching for maximum effect gives his rooster a mouth open to convey savage defiance.

I have studied photos of flying pheasants. Early in the flush, a pheasant's wing and tail feathers are distorted grotesquely by the violence of their effort. The tails of most flying cocks are no neater than a teenager's bed. This is especially true of older roosters, whose long tails whip and billow in flight. Flying cocks have smooth heads, with the pinnae rarely visible. They may bend their necks early in the flush, but once up and under way they point their beaks where they are headed (an arched neck would not be aerodynamic). Their beaks are usually closed, which implies they can cackle with closed mouths.

A pheasant on the ground is remarkably quick, as many hunters have learned to their dismay. A pheasant biologist friend and I once calculated that a cripple with two good legs can run at least sixteen miles an hour. That's slower than the top speed of a hunting dog or a conditioned athlete in track cleats, but faster than just about any hunter in field boots lugging a shotgun.

Sprinting roosters move with a curious high stepping gait, something like a harness trotting horse. Though their legs are short, they clip along at near top speed over broken ground and through vegetation. I know only one hunter who has run down a wing-tipped cripple, and he is built like a rooster, with long legs and muscles as tough as whang leather.

Pheasants aren't built for high or long flights. They usually flush to a height of less than thirty yards. A typical flight is under three hundred yards long, though distances vary greatly with circumstances. While ringnecks have been known to fly three miles, such long flights are extremely unusual.

The outdoor writers of my youth taught us that roosters tower nearly straight up, then suddenly shift into level flight. They further explained there is a magic moment of pause when the rooster "shifts gears." In that split second a cock is a sitting target, they said, and that's when we were told to shoot.

This myth was perpetuated by armchair experts who studied each other's copy instead of pheasants. I've watched enough videos to confirm field experience. For roosters as for airplanes, the laws of physics impose limits on climb angles. Steep angles are inefficient. Roosters slant upward at a moderate angle, gradually level off and then begin the flap-glide-flap sequence that precedes landing. There is no sharp break in the flow of their flight, nor do they stop to shift gears. (And if they did, it would be a stupid time to shoot: when a moving target suddenly and momentarily becomes motionless.)

Pheasants are known as "slow" fliers. Yet they've been clocked at forty-eight miles an hour flying in still air. A rooster flying with a prairie wind is the fastest target an upland hunter will ever see, and I don't believe it is possible to shoot too far ahead of such a bird.

What *is* slow is a rooster's flush. Quail and grouse can't match a pheasant's best speed, but they seem to pop their clutches on the takeoff, hitting top speed within a few wing beats. Not so the rooster, who suffers from a less favorable weight to wing surface ratio. He labors for speed on the takeoff, cussing as he chops a path into the sky.

Yet the rooster is no sitting target. I've timed flushing pheasants in videos. From the moment a rooster begins to flap, it is usually about a second or two before he is up at a safe shooting height. Between seconds two and three, he covers as much as fifteen yards, and that is the time when you must shoot. Later is usually too late.

Most hunters can raise a gun and crack off a shot in just over a second. A hunter shooting as quickly as possible will usually miss or mutilate a close flusher, which might typically be inside twenty yards. The shot should be taken in that precious second when many roosters are moving from twenty yards out to thirty-five yards from the gun.

These are general figures, but instructive. A rooster flushing at close range can be beyond shotgun range in about four seconds. The bird is in ideal shotgun range for a second or a second and a half. The essence of pheasant shooting is making the best use of that brief moment that divides the too-close from the too-far rooster.

My observation convinces me that roosters flush differently after they've had brushes with hunters. A late-season cock who has heard the howl of birdshot near him often flushes low to the ground. I assume such birds are hell-bent on putting distance between them and the gun. Flushing low moves them forward faster because they aren't pouring as much energy into climbing.

Not much is known about the senses of pheasants. Most pheasant research has been directed at habitat, management, and population dynamics.

Though everything in print says pheasants have no sense of

smell, they probably do. Scientists have just recently learned
that birds have all the apparatus of olfaction. Italian researchers
have shown some birds use the sense of smell while migrating,
sniffing their way home like salmon nosing through ocean cur-
rents to find their home stream. Nobody knows to what extent
the sense of smell is developed in pheasants, whether they use
it, or how they use it.

Pheasants have keen vision. The eyes of a pheasant are set
on the sides of its head, the better to see predators with. They
probably have a small area of three-dimensional vision directly
in front. Scientists estimate a pheasant can see trouble approaching from nearly all directions of the compass, having a
tiny "blind spot" directly behind his head. Vision is most precise directly to each side of the bird's head. A pheasant studying a threatening object will regard it sideways rather than
facing it. Pheasants, like most birds, have excellent color vision.

Some authorities say pheasant vision is about as acute as human vision, while others believe it is much more so. Raptors
and turkeys are said to have vision equivalent to a human with
binoculars. Pheasant vision is probably not that keen, though
the birds likely see better than we can. This whole area seems
not to have been studied.

Birds use visual information more creatively than people suppose. Sea gull researchers wear masks when they steal eggs to
study; if they don't, the gulls later attack them relentlessly.
Turkeys in laboratory studies recognize individual faces and are
nervous when approached by humans not wearing the lab coats
worn by the people they trust.

Though penned pheasants fear all humans, they have a limited tolerance for the person who feeds them. A man who raises
pheasants once hired a helper. The hired man dressed in the
jacket and hat of the birds' usual feeder. When he approached
the pen, the pheasants recognized the fraud and went berserk.

It isn't unreasonable to speculate that pheasants use visual cues to identify hunters. The birds might recognize the farmer who usually works their fields. They very likely learn to distinguish between a man in bib overalls on a tractor and a man in blaze orange carrying a gun. A friend hunts pheasants in snow wearing the white camouflage of winter fox hunters. He says he can approach roosters more closely by blending with the surroundings.

Pheasants probably use vision most to elude avian predators, especially when they are exposed. The sense of hearing is most important for evading ground predators such as coyotes or hunters.

In cover, pheasants rely heavily on hearing to keep a safe distance from danger. When hunters follow roosters in weeds, it is the sense of hearing the birds use to monitor the position, speed, and direction of their pursuers. Get down on your belly in good cover sometime. How far can you see? How many inches?

Hunters know that pheasant flushes are usually triggered by what the birds hear, not what they see. By contrast, prairie grouse typically flush when they see something threatening. Two classic ways to flush a rooster are to make a loud noise or to stop making noise altogether. Either tactic can panic a bird whose security depends on hearing.

The pheasant's sensitivity to vibrations extends beyond the limitations of information they receive through their ears. Birds have pressure receptors, called Herbst corpuscles, which respond to vibrations and slight changes in pressure. These receptors are often on the feet, tongue, and featherless portions of the head. They extend "hearing" into a region not sensed by humans.

Little is known about this sensory capability in pheasants. Pheasants have been used in Japan to detect the subtle vibrations that are thought to precede earthquakes. Alas, though many anecdotes suggest pheasants perceive inaudible vibrations, scientists apparently have not yet studied the matter.

Thus the hunter is obliged to speculate. Experienced hunters have often seen pheasants detect the presence of stationary hunters when it seemed obvious the birds could neither see nor hear them. I suspect—but cannot prove—pheasants can perceive vibrations in the earth made by a man standing still but shifting his weight. Does this seem farfetched? Remember, several species of birds are so sensitive to vibrations they can perceive earthworms wriggling under several inches of soil.

If you visit the city parks of Minneapolis on a spring day, you will see something marvelous. Canada geese live there. They graze upon park grass and raise their goslings within feet of secretaries jogging in Lycra suits and elderly couples out giving the family schnauzer his constitutional. These geese accept Cheetos tossed to them. They seem "tame."

However, each goose has around it a circle of fear, a threshold of anxiety. You can approach one so long as you remain beyond that threshold. If you violate that space the goose will waddle into the water, honking protests of your manners. The circle of fear is larger for adult humans than for children, although even toddlers with dimpled knees are not allowed too close. Watch a goose long enough and you'll see it protect its threshold with precision that can be measured in inches.

Around each pheasant there is also a circle of fear. The world is full of creatures that eat young pheasants and even a few predators that can take an adult. Pheasants must stay a safe distance from predators on the ground. Yet pheasants are not exceptionally evasive or rapid fliers. Since some of their deadliest enemies attack from the air, pheasants are understandably reluctant to expose themselves by flying to escape danger.

Instead, pheasants use a combination of mobility and concealment to avoid approaching trouble. They fly only when they must. Mostly they skulk, sneak, or run when a predator threatens to violate their circles of fear. Whatever the limita-

tions a pheasant's brain might have, it is a superb computer
for calculating angles of pursuit and evasion. When you zig,
they zag.

Throughout their short and hazardous lives, pheasants are
continually tested by hawks, foxes, owls, coyotes, cats, and
other predators. Combining learning with instinct, each bird
develops tactics for survival.

Humans differ radically from the other predators pheasants
know. Humans frequently hunt in gangs, employ associates
with keen noses, and carry weapons that make them dangerous
at great range. A bird that has learned strategies for avoiding
single predators armed with teeth or talons—both close-range
weapons—is poorly prepared to deal with this new type of
predator when it explodes into his world in fall.

On opening day, pheasants have a circle of fear and a set of
tactics designed to elude conventional predators. This is particularly true of juvenile roosters, who outnumber the oldsters by
as many as six to one. When kicked up, they fly directly to the
most secure cover in the area, even if doing so sends them past
the guns. Sometimes they fly up to a tree or shrub. Juveniles
often skulk until they lose their nerve and flush right at the feet
of the hunter.

Hunters sometimes joke about these "stupid" birds. The
jokes are stupid; the birds are not. Pheasants weren't born
knowing what a shotgun can do at forty yards. They are simply
using smart tactics against foxes and other ground predators.
The result is a short-lived flurry of easy hunting that typically
accounts for half the roosters shot all season.

Hunters often complain of a "new breed" of pheasant that
runs instead of sitting for a flush as they supposedly once did.
Presumably, earlier generations of hunters shot all the sitters,
leaving only runners to pass on their genes. But if today's bird
is genetically rearranged this way, roosters would all run wildly

on opening day. They don't. Experienced pheasants run because they have learned from experience. We shouldn't be-
grudge them appropriate respect for that.

Perhaps the most impressive of a rooster's senses is his sense
of tactics. And it is hard to account for.

The pheasant is simply not a quarry you would expect to be
overpoweringly intellectual. In the words of my favorite natu-
ralist author, John Madson, "When they passed out brains, the
chicken clan wasn't at the head of the line." Most fall pheasants are only about six months old. And, after all, pheasants are
just *birds*. They don't read books on field tactics or study video
tapes of hunter strategies.

Pheasants have small brains, as I once learned by autopsying
a rooster. The brain is divided into two units that lie on either
side of a bony divider. Each half is about the size of a lima
bean. When you take away those portions of the brain devoted
to controlling physical functions and the mechanics of sight and
flight, there isn't a whole lot of gray matter left to hatch the
schemes that make hunters look silly.

Ah, but they sure manage, don't they?

When hunters say roosters get "educated" or "gunwise,"
some scientifically trained folks become agitated. "Tut tut,"
they protest. "Mustn't talk about animals as if they were little
people! We can't really say that birds *learn*, can we? That's the
old Anthropomorphic Fallacy."

With all due respect, that opinion is a pasture pattie gar-
nished with road apples. Roosters adapt and change. They
learn. Every veteran pheasant hunter knows this. If scientists
can't deal with such an obvious fact, the problem is theirs, not
ours. I'm ready to meet them halfway. Any biologist willing to
bumble around in the weeds behind me with a note pad some
fall is welcome to come. I might be able to use him as a blocker
from time to time.

*   *   *

The central paradox of pheasant hunting is that the sport requires you to force a rooster to do something it does not want to do, namely to flush near a predator. The bird does not want you near him. The bird does not want to fly. He damn well doesn't want to *fly near you*.

Early in the season, young roosters aren't as adverse to flushing near people as they become. The first inclination of young roosters—which category, remember, includes almost all roosters—is to skulk, hunkering to let danger pass. When a young rooster skulks but finds hunters drawing uncomfortably near, he fairly readily takes to the air. Such birds do not last long, nor does the easy hunting they offer.

True pheasant hunting has to do with what follows when the easy birds are gone. With today's bird and hunter numbers, true pheasant hunting begins a day or two into the season. Hunting pressure changes the game day by day, causing roosters to rely increasingly upon sneaking, running, and flushing out of gunshot to keep away from hunters. They no longer have much faith in skulking, though skulk they will if trapped where they can no longer run. Mostly they slink around to keep hunters outside their thresholds of anxiety.

Even before the opening weekend dust settles, cocks get canny. They learn to go where hunters don't go and move in ways few hunters can follow. Yet so long as they resort to concealment and evasive maneuvering, they can be hunted. Hunters with good dogs and sound tactics can take a certain share of these roosters. Good hunters savor this time above all, when their competence is tested and occasionally rewarded. The pheasants are behaving like pheasants, and each one must be earned by hunting hard and smart.

Some pheasants make it to another level, becoming unhuntable. These birds simply refuse to tolerate people anywhere near them. Unhuntable roosters run wildly or flush at enormous distances when men with guns appear. And unless something exceedingly unlucky happens, these birds survive. Nobody knows how many close calls it takes to make a cock unapproachable. I'd guess any rooster that succeeds in beating hunters on four or five encounters is, practically speaking, unhuntable. Maybe three.

Obviously, pheasants have a few advantages going their way in the contest between hunter and hunted.

One big thing the pheasants have going their way is pheasant cover. The great difficulty of grouse hunting is not impossible birds but impossible cover; the great difficulty of pheasant hunting is both wily pheasants and tortuous pheasant cover. You do not lure a rooster onto your ground to hunt him. You go to his ground, and his ground is normally some paradigm of chaos constructed from equal parts of water, muck, and man-eating weeds. A friend of Kathe's once accompanied me to learn what pheasant hunting was like. We were soon thrashing about in the middle of a vast marsh, ankle deep in cold water, under phragmites that loomed twice our height. Louise giggled at the insanity of it. "I never guessed people *went* into such places!" Mostly they don't, which is why roosters do.

Secure cover is a pheasant's first line of defense against carnivores. Heavy cover hides the birds and can even shield their scent from dogs. Roosters can sprint through hellholes of raspberry vines or walls of springy vegetation so thick a dog bounces off it. Deep in weeds, a pheasant hears each footstep of approaching danger, calculating its distance, direction, and speed.

Because hunters come as strangers to pheasant cover, we forget how much time the birds spend there and how attentive they are to minute features of the land and its vegetation. Pheasants use that knowledge to stay alive every waking hour of their lives. Cockbirds can dash through tunnels in the grass only they know about. If there is a tiny pucker in the ground, a pheasant knows it and uses it as an avenue of escape, oozing along as low as a snake. A cock knows his turf.

Experienced pheasants use their terrain creatively to frustrate those who would eat them. Along the McClusky Canal in North Dakota, flushed roosters glide across the canal where they've learned predators cannot follow. The smart way to hunt them would be to follow your dog while toting a canoe. On a farm I know in western Iowa, every startled pheasant dives over the neighbor's fence, the one festooned with *No Hunting* signs. Pogo and I once hiked around a lake rimmed with weeds on a public hunting area. We never saw a pheasant. A fighter jet flew by, obnoxiously low. His sonic boom provoked a chorus of outraged cackling from two dozen roosters. I had to laugh. Every bird was on the other side of the management area fence . . . the safe, private land side.

I once observed pheasants in the act of learning about hunting. We were on Indian land in South Dakota in a year of exceptionally low bird numbers. Our party shot six old roosters for each youngster, a totally upside-down age ratio. Old roosters are usually as hard to pin down as smoke. Not these guys. The Indians hadn't allowed hunting in these fields previously, so we confronted a freak of nature: old, innocent roosters. Cock after cock sat for the flush as tamely as any hen. Wouldn't Spook have had a party there!

The best cover was a series of wrinkly draws that led from a level plain down to the Missouri River. Each draw started as a crease in the prairie that deepened and widened as it neared the river, where the weeds grew thicker and taller. We formed a line of four hunters that drove parallel to the river, slicing across the draws at right angles.

On the first day we found our birds in the lowest, wettest ground where cattails loomed over a man's head and mud sucked at every bootstep. I dropped two roosters in the river that day. The shooting was almost too easy if we stood on the sides of the draws and turned our flushing dogs loose in the cattails. With their first several wing beats, the roosters were climbing closer to our muzzles.

The second day was harder. More cocks flushed wild, and they surprised us by coming up from the buckbrush, kochia, and switchgrass in the middle portions of the draws. We shot half as many birds in the draws as we had the day before.

By the third day, the riverside cocks were no longer naive and approachable. Hens still flew from low areas, but all the long-tailed birds were in gramma and needlegrass at the top ends of the draws. Though that cover was thin, roosters could make safe exits from the high ground. Many flushed out of range from the far sides of the draws; we'd hear the rattle of wings and the bird would be up head-high for a second or two before cresting the hill. It was time to look elsewhere for roosters we hadn't educated.

We had been educated a little, too. Battlewise roosters, especially birds busted from thick weeds by dogs, learn the hazard of being trapped in low spots. Two days were enough to show those pheasants they could no longer count on the protection of the weeds that had offered security all their lives.

Consider that for a moment. How many humans could switch strategies so quickly and effectively if the pet survival tricks they'd acquired in a lifetime were foiled two days in a row? If roosters hunted us as cleverly as they elude us, how long would we last?

PRAIRIE ROOSTERS OF BOTH KINDS

• 5 •

Some roosters seem to flush inch by inch, going up slowly as the bird flogs its bulk into the sky. This was such a bird. First his head came out of the grass, then his russet chest, then his tail. Then more and more tail.

As it turned out, my first South Dakota pheasant was a prairie rooster of the second kind. He was too contrary to be where a pheasant should be and I was too dumb to go where a pheasant hunter should go. So it was fated we should meet.

I was totally intimidated by my first view of South Dakota prairie habitat. Where I grew up, a patch of weeds larger than an acre or two was "real big cover." Now Kathe and I stood at the crest of a bluff peering out over four square miles of continuous vegetation. Strange country, too. It reminded me of an

African savannah, or the moors of Scotland with the purple sucked out.

At first we had no idea of where to find pheasants. By day's end we knew enough to concentrate our efforts on the low ground where a grassy plain merged with a hashy mess of riverside willows and cattails. But in those first minutes we were just-off-the-boat naive, so we walked a monster draw in high country. We didn't know the high draws were sharptail country, no place to find a rooster.

We'd hardly begun the descent when Brandy's body language changed from "I'm *so* excited!" to "I'm so excited about *this bird!*" She glided through the grass, head low to work the intoxicating current of scent, her lithe body thrumming with tension. I chugged behind, wondering what Brandy had going in this lovely but bizarre landscape. Perhaps a red grouse.

Instead it was a pheasant, a prairie rooster of the second kind. When Brandy delivered him to me I saw he was an ancient cock with a tail like a spear and ten-penny nails for spurs. This bird would be as tender on the table as baked owl.

America once had two prairies.

The tallgrass prairie began where the Big Woods stopped in western Indiana and extended westward through Illinois and Iowa, ending just inside the eastern borders of the Dakotas and Nebraska. This was the land of big bluestem, a plant that grew eight feet tall; pioneers reported they could knot strands of big bluestem over a horse's back. This was the genial prairie of Laura Ingalls Wilder, a land of asters, gentians, lupines, blazing stars, coneflowers, daisies, Turk's cap lilies, and pasqueflowers.

That prairie is now gone. The tough sod beneath big bluestem covered rich soil that is watered by moist air from the Gulf of Mexico. Wherever big bluestem once grew you now find vast fields of corn. The old tallgrass prairie became the world's most productive grainery.

To the west of it was a region that frightened many early settlers and should have frightened off more. The shortgrass and mixed-grass prairie lay between the Rockies and the tallgrass prairie. It was and is a land of relentless wind, cacti, low grasses, little moisture, and few trees. This is the Great Plains, sometimes called the Great American Desert because it lies in the rain shadow of the Rockies. It is a lonely, empty land, although not without its own haunting beauty.

Today on the old shortgrass prairie, tumbleweeds go spinning past derelict buildings erected by homesteaders who tried to wrest crops from the poor, arid soil. Tried and failed. Corn grows here only when artificially supported by irrigation. The most productive Great Plains soils sustain milo, sunflowers, and strains of wheat imported from the steppes of Russia.

Ian Frazier, in *The Great Plains,* has called this place a "time park" because it resists change. You still can see ruts worn by the creaking wheels of prairie schooners. Buttes described by Lewis and Clark stand unaltered. The ravines and knolls where the warriors of Gall, Sitting Bull, and Crazy Horse crushed Custer and his Seventh Cavalry troopers would be instantly recognizable to those fighters if their ghosts could return today.

This is the land we still call prairie.

The South Dakota biologist I interviewed had no sense of poetry. My phrase—"prairie roosters"—rasped in his ear like a rock scratching glass. He hastened to correct me. Prairie grouse live on prairies, he said. Pheasants are farmland birds.

Yet, I asked, aren't pheasants moving their range westward? When I was a kid, pheasants flourished in the agricultural heartland, the domain of King Corn. My father and I hunted farms tended by rotund Scandinavians in seed caps and galoshes. Lately my best pheasant hunting has been on windswept plains on land worked by lean, squinty-eyed ranchers wearing cowboy hats and saddle-stitched boots.

It is true, conceded the biologist, that pheasants have expanded their range westward. That's because row crop farming itself has moved west. Construction of the Missouri River reservoirs brought water to the thirsty prairies, allowing maize to raise its head where once little bluestem held sway. Pheasants, because they are farmland wildlife, have followed the westward march of King Corn.

Well okay, I said. But aren't there some pheasants way up in the hills, roosters that have never seen a cornfield, cocks somehow making a go of it in sharptail land among coyotes and prairie rattlers?

He paused. Oh, there might be a *few* such birds. He called them "overflow populations."

I call them prairie roosters of the second kind.

It is, of course, the ordinary prairie rooster that most people hunt. And don't get me wrong. He is one hell of a bird.

He is the farmland pheasant, the corn country cock, the saucy character who makes his living from scraps of waste from America's great agricultural machine. He sees people every day, hates them every day, and every day contrives to take personal advantage of their activities.

In South Dakota, his range extends west until just past the Missouri River. There it stops except where rivers extend wavering root-like fingers into West River country. Where you find water in that country you will find row crops and weeds, and somewhere among row crops and weeds you'll find prairie roosters of the first kind. Our dogs have retrieved dozens of pheasants from rivers and cattle ponds, so you know we hunt close to water. We also find birds along the weedy fringes of center-pivot irrigation wheels, in marshes, stock dams, or creekbeds. Wherever wet ground and farmland exist together, prairie roosters of the first kind will be slinking nearby, adding a riotous splash of color to land men have contrived to make uniform and drab.

I have a romantic fascination for prairie roosters of the second kind.

Now, if I *were* a pheasant, I'm sure I'd live in the lowlands, gobble all the corn I could find, skulk by day in irrigation ditches, and sleep in farmhouse shelterbelts. That would be the normal, pheasanty thing to do. But if I were such a farm-land pheasant, my heroes would be those long-tailed cowboy roosters on the open prairie where farmers can't farm and pheasants don't rightly belong.

As a hunter, I treasure those birds. While there has never been a tame pheasant, the birds living out of sight of row crops and blue metal silos seem more purely wild. Their crops are full of grasshoppers, snowberries, and all sorts of scraggly wild seeds instead of soybeans destined to be gaveled down at the Chicago Board of Trade. They are the ornery ones who won't stay put, the rebels scrabbling for survival out on the ragged edges of pheasant habitat.

It would please me to report such birds are exceptionally hard to bag. Just the opposite is true. They flush wild in a bad wind, as all pheasants do. Sometimes they run, but not usually very far. They simply don't know human hunters as bitterly well as farmland birds do. Consequently, they're not as evasive as a corn country cock whose tail has been stung with shot.

The hard part of hunting them is the long hiking, since these birds are spread far apart. Walking mile after mile over hills of wind-tossed grass is sometimes lonely and always beautiful. I put in many hours out there with no company except the excellent company of a dog. In that vast grass landscape under the azure dome of sky, my dog and I are two tiny figures, as insignificant as ants. When I walk the concrete canyons of large cities, I feel small and bad; when I walk an empty prairie with a dog, I feel small and good. The world we pass through has been reduced to fundamentals. Grass, sky, and wind. Everything is grass, sky, and wind. And while we are always thrilled to cross paths with a rooster, we don't need that to feel right about what we are doing. Out on the prairie we are free, my friends, as free as it is possible to be in this life.

Four of us once hunted some Sioux reservation land south of Pierre, along the Missouri. It was November, late in the season, and pheasants were not abundant. But the land was big and lovely in that special forlorn loveliness of a tawny prairie under stone-colored skies, with winter so close we could feel its hard breath on our necks.

Down low by the feet of the river, cattails, Sudan grass, and bulrushes grew in the rich river mud. Pheasants were there. Hunting the marshes was jungle warfare, and we toted guns one-handed to leave a hand free to claw passage through the weeds. We got close, heart-attack flushes there, and the cocks our dogs retrieved were wet.

A number of gullies and draws trailed down from the higher country to meet the river flats. These were filled with snowberry, chokeberry, plum thickets, and switchgrass. Pheasants were there, too.

The magic country, though, was a grand table of level land above the river. This huge plain hadn't been cultivated for decades and sported a rich growth of little bluestem, gramma, wheatgrass, and needlegrass. Here and there, decrepit shelterbelts held naked branches against the sky. Literally everything our eyes could see was bird cover, none of it much more attractive than the rest. It was goofy, brainless hunting. There was no more reason to walk one direction than another. Yet if a man and dog set sail over that sea of billowing grass, tacking left and right to use the wind, they found birds.

Sometimes the dogs bounced up flocks of chunky buff and

white birds that chopped their wings vigorously, scolding us for disturbing them. Those were sharptails.

Sometimes we'd kick up a similar bird, only it would be a single, darker in hue and silent in flight. Those were prairie chickens.

And sometimes the dogs would gallop through the high grass, questing left and right to test the margins of the envelope of scent. The trail would sometimes bend right or left but rarely did it go long. It ended when a dog dove with snapping teeth into the grass. Then up would come a bird with a streaming tail, hurling curses at us with the eloquence of an old pirate making his last stand.

Those were magnificent birds, rare trophies, prairie roosters of the second kind.

BLIZZARD ON THE
RACE TRACK

—— • 6 • ——

When I woke up, I didn't know where I was. And, holy cow, what *was* that noise? It sounded like London during the Blitz.

Slowly, consciousness burned away the mists of sleepy confusion. Oh, yeah. I was in a sleeping bag on the floor of a deserted South Dakota farmhouse. Brandy was curled beside me, a paw tucked demurely over her freckled nose. Bill was in the next room. But what was that noise? With each bang, the walls shook and crumbs of plaster trickled down. Glass panes rattled in sloppy window frames in a way that suggested we were in an earthquake. I ventured timidly out of the bag.

The window seemed to have been spray-painted white by vandals in the night. When I found an opening to peer through, I could recognize nothing. Then I understood. We were in a blizzard. The wind howled so maniacally that leafless shrubs strained at their roots. Shelterbelt cottonwoods wrenched side to side like aerobics exercisers. Snow streamed flat across the prairie like something shot from a firehose. Every few seconds, lightning bolts fused earth to sky in a light show from Hell.

Wow. I slid back in the bag, lit a cigar, and found the place marker in my mystery novel. We wouldn't hunt today.

This had been a weird pheasant opener from the start.

Bill and I thought we'd scored a great coup. At a time every motel in South Dakota was booked solid with opening week-end hunters, I was able to rent a cabin at a lakeside resort. Magic words, those: *cabin, lakeside, resort.* We would clean limits of pheasants by the dancing blue waters in front of the cabin, then sit pensively with glasses of whiskey while the setting sun dropped behind the far shoreline in a glory of flame orange.

Ah, but life is full of surprises. The "resort" turned out to be a trailer ghetto full of shabby motor homes. Our "cabin" had not been left unlocked for us, as promised, so we had to roust the proprietor from his bed; he shuffled out in socks and under-shorts, reached through the broken window, and opened the door from the inside. The cabin was illuminated by three naked light bulbs dangling from the cardboard ceiling. Coil springs protruded through the plastic upholstery of the furniture. The kitchen tap emitted amber clots of goo instead of water. Throughout the night, burly animals conducted orgies or wars or both inside the cabin walls. Daylight arrived to show us the "lake" was a shallow basin of slimy, blurping algae, almost thick enough to walk upon. I expected at any moment to see some new life form come crawling up out of that primordial ooze.

Our hunting was an extension of the resort experience. The summer had been so wet farmers didn't dare take field machinery into muddy fields to harvest crops. The pheasants were scattered throughout the standing corn where we had no chance of shagging them out. The only rooster we saw taken all day was ground-sluiced by some Alabama boys who never left the comfort of the velour seats in their conversion van to pot the bird. Man, it has to be *loud* to touch off a shot inside a van like that!

That evening Bill and I chewed some rubbery cafe chow mein and discussed our options. "We've got to get out of here," said Bill, with feeling. I agreed. "Out of here and clear away from all this standing corn." We were up early in the morning. We paid up and told the resort man we had to cancel the rest of our reservation. My grandmother had died, poor dear, most unexpectedly.

For three hours we drove south and west on highways lined with discouraging walls of standing corn. Gradually, the land changed, becoming flatter and drier. Corn began sharing the landscape with milo. Farms became bigger, the farm homes more widely dispersed. We had crossed out of the old tallgrass prairie into the Great Plains. "This looks better," I finally said. "More crops down."

Bill studied a map of South Dakota public hunting areas. "Here's a possibility," he said. "It's big, about half a section. Should be a bird out there somewhere. Hang a right in two miles." Soon my red station wagon humped into the corner parking lot of the management area. It was big all right, though more uniform than is ideal. The ground was almost tabletop flat and covered overall with thigh-high wheatgrass. "We might as well start here as anywhere," I said. "It all looks the same."

We had barely closed our guns when Brandy's head snapped down and she bustled northward. Bill and I loped behind. Brandy paused to puzzle out a confusing puddle of scent, then shot away again. Twice her course curved, giving the humans a deeply appreciated chance to catch up with the galloping springer. Brandy finally did a curling maneuver, staring into the grass with her *"thumb yer safeties"* expression. Bill dropped the rooster that flashed up near him.

"Good shot," I said, panting. "Good dog work," said Bill as he twisted to drop the bird in his game bag. "Uh, speaking of Brandy, where is she?" Brandy was charging through the wheatgrass again, noisily sucking scent. We ran. She ran. The bird ran and ran and ran. About the time Bill and I were ready to give up, Brandy slammed on the brakes and maneuvered cautiously for the flush. Another rooster.

I wheezed as I accepted the fragrant gift from Brandy. Leaning on his Citori, Bill said, "This is crazy. I wonder what Steve Grooms, author of *Modern Pheasant Hunting*, would do in a situation like this." I shook my head. "Bill, I keep saying you've got to develop more cynicism about outdoor writers. They are knaves, fools, and drunks, and the truth is not in them." I added darkly, "Anyway, I've heard stories about that Grooms character. If he was here he'd be running as stupidly as we've been, only I'm sure he couldn't keep up with us."

"Where's Brandy?"

"She's right . . . uh oh! *Run!*"

The rest is quickly told: two hours, eight chases, six rooster flushes, six shells fired, six retrieves. And every bird ran like a cat with four soup cans tied to his tail. It was the most aerobic pheasant hunt I've known. We had done a 10K marathon in shell vests and boots, toting over-unders. Our shortest chase might have been sixty yards, the longest three times that distance.

Back in the car, Bill drew an arrow on the map toward the management area and carefully penned in the name we'd given it: "The Race Track."

"Jim Layton should have seen this," I said as we drove off in search of a place to sleep. Jim had been our pheasant hunting host in central Iowa for years. A canny pheasant man, Jim was also an incurable optimist. He'd squint at the skies each morning and drawl, "Awww, it looks super. I bet them ol' roosters will be settin' real tight today." And he was wrong every time. Every damn time. Whether the skies were gray, blue, or chartreuse with pink polka dots, we never once found Jim's late season Iowa roosters willing to hold tight.

Following a lead from a kind motel lady, Bill and I drove to a farm that might be able to accommodate us. There we met a pleasant middle-aged couple of Dutch descent, their faces etched by years of exposure to prairie weather. He had a farmer's tan. The skin on his neck was as dark as liver while his forehead bore the sickly pale shape of a duck's bill, a negative image of his cap. He called himself a *"dry-land* farmer."

Next to their property was an abandoned farmhouse, a forlorn shell that held silent memories and no furniture. If we didn't mind sleeping on the floor, we were welcome. We weren't told the couple's hospitality would include a visit each morning with fresh-baked chocolate chip cookies and a steaming thermos of coffee.

We spent two happy days camping in the farmhouse. Then the blizzard hit.

I awoke the second time about mid-morning, *Trent's Last Case* folded over my nose like a pup tent. Bill and I peered out the dining room window at an eerie moonscape. My station wagon was a Styrofoam caricature of a car. Every tree seemed to have been sprayed white on its northwest side. Wind buffeted the farmhouse and keened around the gables while the torrent of snow spilled laterally over the prairie.

"We aren't going hunting, are we?" asked Bill. I laughed, "Is that some kind of trick question or something? We'd never even make it out the driveway. The Ford has crummy traction." "Yeah," Bill agreed, "it would be miserable out there, anyway."

I returned to the sleeping bag and Trent. Industrious Bill waterproofed his boots and oiled his Citori.

Minutes later we were both back with noses pressed to the dining room window like kids outside a candy store. "I've been thinking," I said. "Me too," said Bill. "We'll surely end up in a ditch." "Yeah, but if we don't . . . ." "If we don't, man, it could be *something*."

We hacked snow off the car with an old broom whose whiskers were all worn off. The snow was almost axle deep. To get on the gravel county road we'd have to punch through a snowy uphill grade. I rocked the car, laying down a track, then floored the accelerator while Bill pushed. With tires whining like poltergeists, the Fairmount slewed left and right, faltered, then popped onto the gravel. We'd take breakfast in town, then attempt to reach The Race Track.

Small town cafes in pheasant country all look pretty much the same, all wonderful, and you feel as much at home in them as you do in your own kitchen. In the front window is a placard cheering on the local football team: "Spear 'em, Spartans!" The breakfast aromas of coffee and bacon and yeasty rolls float amicably over the quiet, steady fragrance of the griddle. On the formica counter, glass cases tempt you with fresh-baked pies and pastries that leak glimmering pools of calories. The menus are plastic with hand-typed inserts, some entrees misspelled. Pale red posters stapled to the walls advertise farm auctions and estate sales, with frequent mentions of "antiques" that you suspect are just old, cheap things that have had a hard life. The paper placemats carry the same improbable wildlife scenes that you've eaten upon since you began habituating such cafes some thirty-five years ago. A kelly green bass with a mouth the size of a garbage can leaps for a dragonfly suspended in a fluorescent orange sky. At one table, large-bodied men guzzle coffee from ivory porcelain mugs and practice the art of understatement. They bang dice in a leather cup on the table to see who gets stuck with the bill, laughing the comfortable laugh of men who have known each other all their lives. And if you are lucky, your waitress will be a silver-haired woman, broad of beam, with smile creases radiating from her eyes. She raised six children and worked the farm with her husband before his first heart attack, when they retired to the Victorian gingerbread home on the edge of town. And you see it in her eyes as she comes around with the coffee: she has spent her life serving food to men as an expression of love. This, for her, is not employment. This, for her, is religion.

The storm had taken down local power lines, so the darkened cafe was jammed with folks clucking about the weather and relishing the novelty of ordering a breakfast that didn't require electricity. We could have coffee, eggs, and pecan rolls but, sorry, no toast. Toast was electric.

At a nearby table, four farmers in bib overalls and seed caps played a game of whist by the shuddering light of a candle. One studied our hunting garb with friendly amusement. He cackled, "Hee, hee, hee! I guess it ain't your day, boys!" I said, "Matter of fact, we think this is our day." He frowned. "You're not hunting pheasants in *this* weather!" "We're going to give it a try," said Bill. The farmer rolled his eyes. We'd made him a happy man. He had a story to share with everyone he'd meet, and in a small town stories are a more precious currency than folding money.

On the road to The Race Track we passed three vehicles abandoned in crazy postures in the white ditches. Twice we nearly joined them. There were, of course, no other hunters at The Race Track. I seriously doubted there were hunters afoot anywhere in the county that morning.

The blizzard roared relentlessly. To be heard, I had to shout directly in Bill's ear. Just getting out of the car and loading guns was misery. Even Brandy suffered visibly, shivering while we suited up. Bill wore literally every item of clothing he'd brought for the trip, including pajamas, underwear, a two-piece rain suit, and two hats jammed on his head at once. Nothing would have been enough.

About twenty yards from the car, a silver buffaloberry shrub punched through the infinite emptiness of white. It was the only thing I could see that was not snow. I directed Brandy toward it with a flick of my hand. Brandy stuck her head under the shrub, then popped up to stare at me with eyes wide with amazement. There was a little snow cave under the buffalo-berry. Brandy slapped the ground twice with both paws. Nothing happened. She ran to the far side of the shrub and popped at the ground again. The rooster was the very picture of misery when he crawled out. He squatted and flushed the only direction he could fly, straight down the wind. Bill's shot tumbled him.

The next moment is one of my favorite memories of Brandy. After a decade of hunting pheasants in her own way, she totally reinvented the sport. One rooster sufficed to teach Brandy the novel reality of this situation. She rose on her hind legs, fore-paws dangling like a Kodiak bear. Straining to make herself tall, Brandy peered around for another bush. There was one fifty yards to the west. Brandy plowed straight to it, not using her nose, not quartering, and jammed her head under the shrub. That one held a hen. Then Brandy lifted, bear-like, scanning for another shrub.

Each time she rooted under a bush, Bill and I arranged ourselves downwind for a shot. The shooting was not as easy as it must sound. We couldn't hear the flushes, and to look upwind toward Brandy was painful. Twice roosters rocketed by us so quickly our frozen hands couldn't react fast enough. A pair of roosters escaped when I peeped upwind too long and got both eyes packed with snow like a vaudeville clown catching a cream pie in his face.

In between bushes we walked backwards with arms wrapped around our guns, gloved hands clamped up under our armpits, looking like two of Napoleon's musketmen in retreat from Moscow. Icicles hung from our moustaches. We could only walk with our backs to the wind, and standing upright was impossible. If we leaned back into it, strong hands of Canadian air supported us at improbable angles. When I had to get rid of my breakfast coffee I was sorely tempted just to let fly down my leg. It would be so warm . . . for a while, anyway.

Some birds refused to fly until Brandy cuffed them around. Once Brandy burrowed out of sight under the snow along a fence. We could trace her progress under the white drifts by the hummocky trail she made, like a mole's runway. She emerged at last with a crippled rooster in her jaws. "He wouldn't have made it through the next night anyway," Bill said. Four times Brandy returned to us with hens, unhurt, in her mouth. From under some buckbrush, Brandy routed out a rooster that zipped past me like a bolt from a crossbow. I turned to take him as a straightaway. That made five in the bag, one to go.

We were walking crablike, sideways to the wind, when I called to Bill. Brandy sat whining on the high gravel road that divided two parts of the management area. The frozen road was so cold she lifted one paw then the other from it. "Brandy wants us to cross," I yelled. Doing that would expose us to the worst of the wind while we negotiated two tricky barbed wire fences. Bill roared in my ear, "Whatever Brandy wants today, she gets!"

As Bill crossed the fence, he came down on top of a hen. Seconds later we heard the harsh metallic two-note rasp of a rooster. A large cock with a broken wing sprinted from a clump of weedy trash, looking impossibly bright like molten copper against the white. Brandy hit him in a tumbling flurry of snow. We were done.

"I don't believe it," said Bill, shaking his two hats. "One thing," I said, "I wish Jim had been here to see this." "Yeah," Bill agreed. "It finally happened. Them ol' roosters were settin' real tight."

The return to the car was an almost pleasant downwind

jaunt. I forgot to put Brandy on heel and only remembered when she waded into the ditch to claw at another buffaloberry bush. After slapping her paws several times, Brandy picked up the rooster that refused to flush. We released him into the whirling oblivion of white, praying he'd soon find a haven somewhere downwind.

A DOG MAN'S TESTAMENT

—————• 7 •—————

Someone has written that a man is either a shooter, a hunter, or a dog man. In that context, I used to be a hunter and now am a dog man. Though I hunted pheasants without dogs for sixteen years, it has become difficult to conceive of the sport without the grinning, muddy presence of a dog.

Hunting pheasants without a dog is like paddling a canoe solo. You might eventually get where you intend to go, but the act lacks logic and grace. And dogless pheasant hunting is often more akin to rowing a boat with one oar.

Hunting without a dog is boring because only one result, seeing a bird, gives your mind data to play with. Seeing no birds, the more common result, is negative information, and that's thin stuff for constructing hypotheses. Logicians have a phrase for that: "Absence of evidence is not evidence of absence." If you see no pheasants, you might be hunting a field devoid of birds. Or maybe all the birds skulked and let you sail by. Or maybe a dozen roosters skipped out the back door of the cover when you walked in the front. You just don't know.

Add a dog to the hunt, and things change. Of course, you'll shoot more birds, but that's not the point. Every step you take with a dog is progress toward comprehending the pattern for the day. If your dog cruises a field without even finding a ghost of old scent, you know no birds are near. While disappointing, that at least is useful information. You can do something about it.

That is not to say dogs automatically make pheasant hunting joyful and productive. Bad hunts without dogs are just frustrating and fruitless. Bad hunts starring misbehaving dogs are agony.

It isn't natural for a dog with strong bird desire to hunt under control. The desire is natural but the control is not. Control must be put in the dog with training and then sustained with diligence, and there is nothing automatic about it. This is especially true of pointing dogs, for they have a more demanding task to perform, casting widely to find pheasants, then contriving to fix those fiddlefooted birds in place.

A number of hunters today seem to regard the English driven pheasant hunt as the ultimate experience life has to offer. I find that very difficult to understand. Could it feel good to kill birds you have done nothing to earn? Could it be fun to kill so many? I'm surely weird. I'd be embarrassed by the political symbolism, standing there like a tweed god while working class lackeys flogged the brush for me. Worse, it would disturb me to kill birds with whom I had no relationship other than shooter to target. But, hell, I said it already. I'm a dog man, not a shooter.

The sport of pheasant hunting has levels of emotional delight never experienced—never even imagined—by those who hunt without dogs. Only the dog owner understands the joy of watching your teammate working his heart out to find birds, sorting out the ambiguous messages of scent, and dealing successfully with one of the world's most elusive and uncooperative game birds. Each point or close flush your dog scores on an experienced rooster is a minor miracle. The birds you kill are not just targets and not strangers, for you have shared a crucial moment with them and have known them wild and free in all their exorbitant, savage beauty. Only by hunting them hard and acknowledging their ferocious will to live do you earn the right to take their lives.

And when it all goes well, when your dog does the difficult and does it with style, what you get isn't a bagged bird but the honor of sharing a moment of penultimate drama starring the dog you love and the bird you love. That is a taste of Heaven, friends, and it's why the dog man hunts. And frankly, most of us kick through one hell of a lot of weeds between glimpses of Heaven.

I don't believe people can learn pheasant hunting by reading books (an uncomfortable notion for someone about to inflict his second such book on the world). That's just not the way we learn anything. We learn from experience. Then, when we have enough experience to be pleasantly confused, reading the right book can organize experience and cast light on some of the murky places.

If you are serious about learning this grand sport, buy the best dog you can afford and three pairs of nylon-faced hunting pants. Train your dog or put him in the hands of someone who can. Then go to the birdiest, weediest spots you know and put the dog down. Walk behind him, listening with care to what he tells you about pheasants. Hunt until your pants have bobwire cuts in the crotch and cuffs frayed until they hold cockleburs like a springer's silky ears. When all your pants are too holey to be worn in the presence of ladies, your dog will have told you most of what you will ever know about pheasant hunting. At that point you can afford to take risks by listening to self-appointed experts such as I. Read a book or some magazine stories about hunting pheasants. You might even rent a video.

But when experts disagree with your dog and your experience, you'll know who to believe.

I believe it was Frank Woolner who said you could always get help if hopelessly lost in grouse woods by yelling something like, "The Vizsla is the finest grouse dog in the world." Instantly you'll be surrounded by hunters ready to punch out your lights for failing to see the obvious supremacy of their chosen breeds. If you survive the discussion, you'll have no end of folks to guide you home.

Dog lovers have a strange preoccupation with breed. American hunters are as disputatious about the "best" breed as folks a century or two ago were about the "right" religious denomination. In that sense, I am devoutly nonsectarian. I've hunted with great goldens, shorthairs, Brittanys, springers, wirehairs, Labs, and English setters. I've also seen individuals from all those breeds that should not have been allowed to survive their misbegotten puppyhoods. No breed has a monopoly on quality.

Few hunters, though they are overly concerned with breed, pay the attention to training and handling they should. American sportsmen believe success is not a thing they must earn but something they can buy (if they are shrewd enough to select the best products). We all have experience buying things, yet few contemporary Americans—even hunters—have much experience training or disciplining animals.

Though I love dogs to a fault, I have prejudices. To my mind, trained dogs are better than untrained dogs. I also believe good dogs—dogs bred with sound bodies, sensitive noses, and happy temperaments—are preferable to badly bred dogs.

Finest of all are those rare animals that draw the best cards in the genetic poker game and are then given a proper education.

I once criticized a buddy who flouted the ambition of marrying a rich woman. Like a heroine in a Harlequin romance, I declaimed that one should marry for love. "Indeed," said my cynical friend, "but you can love a rich one just as well as a poor one." Similarly, you can love a good dog at least as well as a poor one.

Most of us must content ourselves with imperfect dogs. Happily, several factors mellow over the discordant notes in relations between dogs and owners. Time teaches dogs and owners to adapt to each other. After enough years, they come to fit each other like two rough stones carried in the same pocket. It is good our dogs don't hold the unrealistic expectations of us we hold of them.

Opening weekend offers the most productive hunting of all, but you pay a price. Usually there are too many people afield, especially too many once-a-year hunters with primitive field manners. One year Kathe and I opened the season on a crowded public hunting area in western Minnesota. Most folks were polite. But wherever I went I could hear one guy across the way braying like a foghorn, "King, King! You *dumbass* sumbitch! Git your shaggy butt over here!" He apparently belonged to that large school of hunters who theorize it isn't necessary to train a dog if one is prepared to holler loud enough at him in the field.

By some willows, Brandy put up a rooster, and I shot it. She had just picked up the bird when the ground began to shake. Here came a coal black Labrador the size of a beef calf, solid bone between the ears, with a cretinous fixed grin on his lips. This was King, about whom I had heard so much.

King grabbed part of the rooster dangling outside Brandy's mouth. Brandy was a sweet dog in all situations but one. She was fiercely possessive about her birds and would not have surrendered a rooster to a rabid grizzly. King and Brandy squared off, eyeball-to-eyeball, growling like two Top Fuel dragsters revving on the line. My poor rooster stretched thin as the dogs tug-o-warred it.

Just then there arrived a florid man in bib overalls. He waded in, kicked King in the slats, and picked up my noodle-shaped pheasant. In what was obviously a supreme gesture of sportsmanship, he offered it to me, saying peevishly, "Guess I'll let you have this bird although it was my dog what retrieved it."

I grinned all afternoon. Now *there* was a match made in Heaven! I never saw a man and dog who deserved each other so richly.

When Kathe and I determined to buy our first hunting dogs the only thing we knew for certain was which end the food went in and from which end it eventually reappeared. Our only hunting experience was with two Labradors that were so weirdly unlike each other we had no fix on even that breed. So I brought home several library books on dogs.

The more I read, the less I knew. All breeds were described with cliches drawn from the same stock file. Every hunting breed was "lively," "affectionate," and, above all, "intelligent." In fact, *every* dog breed in the books was guaranteed to exhibit exceptional intelligence, like the mythical town where all children are above average. So much indiscriminate praise tended to call in question the standards of the doggy experts. I yearned for less boosterism and more candor: "This breed is as stupid as a stone, but handsome, quite handsome."

We eventually identified preferences. I wanted a Brittany or springer because they were "compact, lively, affectionate, and intelligent." Plus, I read, they were deft with pheasants. Kathe objected, "But they have no tails. If God meant dogs to have no tails, he wouldn't have given them tails."

We next attended a few informal field trials, a disheartening experience. Though the books assured us flushing dogs were "bred to hunt in gun range," we saw many that had obviously been bred to hunt everywhere else. Offsetting that, we witnessed some dandy flushing work from the pointing breeds.

We located a man named Henry who owned a dual champion Brittany and who was eager to show us a great Brit in action. Kathe and I met him at a local shooting preserve. Henry dizzied two chukar partridges and shoved them under some grass. Then it was time for the dual champion to do his thing. He was rather fat and ancient, an old warrior gone to pot, but he knew this scene. He backtracked his master's scent right to the first chukar and went *boiing* on point.

Henry moved in, shouting, "Are you ready, Steve?" "Yes! Of course, I'm ready!" (Actually I was hyperventilating, as I hadn't anticipated this moment of high tension.) Henry kicked the dickens out of the grass. No bird appeared. He yelled again, "Steve, are you ready?" "Yes, dammit, yes! I'm *ready*!" My nerves by this time were like a wine goblet being scrunched in a vise. Suddenly Henry dove on his belly with surprising agility for a senior citizen. He snagged the chukar in one hand and hurled it into the air. I blasted two 12-gauge holes in the sky. The dual champion then beelined to the second dizzy chukar and the whole process repeated itself just as before, with Henry flopping to his belly to launch the bird, except I remember making a weak hit on that bird.

As we drove home, Kathe told me, "You can suit yourself, but I just don't like pointing dogs. Maybe you can get a springer. Me, I'll buy a Lab. They are nice dogs. And they have tails."

Kathe bought Pukka, the supreme jock of dogdom. I paid seventy-five dollars for Brandy, an investment that paid me back with compound interest every day for over fourteen years. And we were happy.

Years later, Kathe and I hunted with Jim Layton on a farm south of Jim's place. That farm had no more cover visible from the road than a tray of kitty litter, but if you knew the place you knew there was a wonderful swale of horseweeds, brome, and switchgrass on the back side. This was after Pukka's death but before puppy Brinka could hunt, so Kathe hunted with Jim behind Archie Bunker, Jim's excellent Brittany, while I chased Brandy from horizon to horizon.

When Archie went rigid along a weedy ditch, Jim let Kathe take the chance. A rooster blazed up and fell to her shot. As Archie made the retrieve, Kathe thought, "I never knew this pointing dog hunting could be so thrilling! I feel a tremendous *buzz*! God, I feel *tingly all over!*" Then Kathe noticed she was holding her shotgun barrels on the hot wire of an electric cattle fence.

That night Kathe told me she had reconsidered the matter and now felt pointing dogs were okay. "You remember when I told you not to buy one? Well, the part I didn't like was where the hunter has to flop on his belly to throw the bird in the air."

I was anxious going into my first pheasant hunting season with Spook. Talking to veteran hunters didn't ease my mind. They all chimed with a single voice, "Whatever you do, don't let a pointing pup anywhere near those damned running roosters. They'll ruin him for life!"

I once witnessed such a thing, and it wasn't pretty. A highly bred young setter stuck her nose in a South Dakota breeze that reeked of pheasant scent. Her eyes altered in a frightening way. Then she lit out to set the Guinness World Record for total pheasants flushed out of range by one setter in a single afternoon. And got it.

In my favor was the fact Spook had been carefully bred by Jim Marti at his Burnt Creek Kennels. Spook was a sensible and precocious pup, with no flightiness in his makeup. I'd also had the wisdom to turn him over to a gifted young trainer, Steve Grossman, before I screwed him up. The chemistry between Spook and Steve was superb. Steve had Spook steady to wing and shot before he was a year old.

Still, I brooded. In all my years with Brandy, we rarely crossed paths with a rooster willing to sit patiently while I walked up to kill him. Most ran, some running so long and hard I had to conclude they'd been born without wings. It made absolutely no sense to hunt a mobile bird with a stationary dog.

Imagine my surprise on Spook's first pheasant trip. He struck a point in some slough grass in a soggy gully below a hill. I humored him by giving the weeds a few desultory kicks, though there was nothing there. Of course. Pheasants run. I was returning to release Spook from his point when I stepped on the rooster. I managed to drop that guy in the act of falling on my butt.

Why hadn't he run?

Why, for that matter, didn't the next several roosters run? I hunted in befuddled bliss as cock after cock sat under Spook's points. In a dry North Dakota creekbed on his second day of pheasant hunting, one of his points produced a pair of scolding roosters. One went with the wind and was a blurry memory before I could mount my gun, but the other made a doomed decision to fly straight against the booming prairie wind. I had time to recite the "Pledge of Allegiance" before firing.

Great. But why hadn't those roosters run?

At season's end I mulled the matter over. So many pheasants had held tight, I concluded, because they didn't have Brandy and me running straight at them with six pounding feet, snorting and wheezing like the hounds of Hell. Though obvious, that fact was one I was slow to grasp.

Of course, some roosters naturally skulk, and those that did found a young setter staring daggers at them. Others sneaked away. Then Spook simply set about finding and pointing them again, and we got a number of those birds, though not all. Some roosters are just determined to run, and many of them made it to safety.

It seems to me now that a cock that insists on running will elude a pointer more often than a flusher because it is easier for the flusher, working with ground scent, to maintain hot contact with the bird. But fewer roosters are firmly predisposed to run than I had thought. Many can be lulled by the less aggressive pursuit of the pointer into slowing down and hiding. And then the pointer nails them. Some pointers, and Spook is one, also learn to hold a point while flowing along with a moving bird. It is called roading, and it is an amazing thing to behold.

Flushing dogs can be trained to stop on the whistle even in the fever of the chase, though that degree of control is not accomplished by many hunters. Everything in the dog's nature says *GO!* I've seen marvelous work by whistle-trained flushers. The hunting results justify the considerable training effort. A stoppable Lab or springer is your best hope when you must contend with racehorse roosters.

I faced other adjustments that first fall with Spook. Steve Grossman believed a pointing puppy should not be asked to retrieve in his first year of contact with wild birds. I felt a little naked knowing I didn't have a retriever to cover for my sloppy shooting. For years I had counted on the fact that if I got a piece of the bird, Brandy would get the rest.

Again, I was pleasantly surprised. I lost two cripples that fall that Brandy probably would have fetched. Of the twenty-three wild pheasants I fired at, all but two died in the air. That's a better clean-kill ratio than I ever managed while dashing behind Brandy. I shot better because I was shooting over points, so things even out.

Another adjustment I've made while hunting with Spook has been to rethink my old ideas about wind. Like all flushers, Brandy worked best with wind in her face, and we went to great lengths to hunt choice bits of cover upwind. I thought the importance of hunting upwind was possibly the only absolute rule in pheasant hunting.

On his fourth day of pheasant hunting, Spook and I were forced to go downwind through a strip of prairie grasses along a canal of North Dakota's infamous Garrison Diversion. Spook hit a point. I whacked the weeds with one boot and learned the bird had vacated the premises. Well, that's what I expect of a rooster approached from the upwind side. Such birds often skip out from a point.

When released, Spook flew downwind. It seemed he knew a bird was loose in front of him and was determined to loop around it to relocate with the wind coming to his nose. I was just about to reprimand him for straying too far away when Spook snapped into a "U." There was no pup foolishness in Spook's expression. He was saying, "He's not just around, Boss. He's *right here!*" I didn't rush to make the flush because I knew that pheasant wouldn't take another step. He thought he was absolutely surrounded by white setters.

Four times on downwind hunts that fall Spook looped downwind of a rooster that ran away from his first point. I don't think he invented this downwind looping technique intellectually but was simply making good use of his legs and the wind. But it was sure pretty to see. Other pointing dog hunters have told me their dogs do the same thing, especially on downwind hunts in strip cover.

My hunting has changed in several ways. Brandy and I were birds of a feather, passionate panting predators who lived to

kill. I still hunt hard and it still means a great deal to me to
hold a rooster in my hand, yet increasingly I find my main satisfaction comes from watching Spook flowing through the cover
and casting spells on the birds.

Each rooster we take means more to me than the birds I used
to take with Brandy. And that's saying a great deal.

JUST THREE SKILLS

—— • 8 • ——

To hunt pheasants successfully, you need just three skills. You must be able to find birds, maneuver them to force a close flush, and then shoot reasonably well. Three skills. That's all! Now, how hard can that be?

Finding pheasants begins as a job of research. By talking to wildlife managers, you learn which general areas hold good numbers of pheasants. You then query more sources, always seeking the most authoritative information available. Remember that some folks have economic incentives to give optimistic reports. If they see five roosters while driving to work, they're apt to report all ten of them when you call asking if you should bring your gun and checkbook to their community in November.

Inform yourself, also, about the accessibility of fields to hunt. Some localities are wealthy in public hunting acres and some are not. Farmers in some regions are suspicious of nonresidents while farmers elsewhere welcome outsiders more readily than local hunters. In some areas you hunt private land only by paying for the privilege. Research tells you these things.

After research, mental games begin. The amount of quality pheasant hunting in America falls woefully short of the demand for it. Many other hunters will learn exactly what you learn about birdy areas, and most of them assume they should hunt where pheasants are most abundant. They forget how many other hunters have the same plan.

Early in the season it often pays to hunt where the greatest number of birds were born. Opening weekend in a birdy land can be paradise. You risk encountering crowds, though, and I'd never hunt the prime zone of the state claiming the best bird numbers that year. You want to go where there are many birds but few hunters—except birds and hunters are almost always found together. If you dodge the hunters you risk missing the bountiful bird populations. Such dilemmas permeate pheasant hunting.

From opening weekend on, smart hunting requires a tricky balancing act. You want to hunt where there are pheasants, yes, but pheasants that can be hunted. With each passing day, hunting pressure in highly publicized regions grinds down bird numbers and turns survivors into spooky will-o'-the-wisps.

Decisions, decisions! Where should you go? I'm a veteran hunter with a great dog, but I'd rather hunt a field holding two uneducated roosters than one with a hundred smart cocks. I spend a lot of time in areas with marginal pheasant numbers.

Now you are actually in the field, still facing the problem of finding pheasants. You must use precious hunting time wisely.

Which areas are most likely to produce cock flushes? I suggest three game plans.

Start by thinking of the pheasant as a *lowland* gamebird. Many of the roosters I've taken have flushed from water. They're not there because they enjoy getting wet. Drive a country road at sunrise and you'll see pheasants outside the cover, protecting their feathers from the jewels of water adorning each blade of grass. Pheasants hang out near water because they find the rankest and most secure weeds down where water mixes with soil to promote luxuriant vegetative growth.

I came to love marsh hunting back when Brandy hit the cover like a white tornado. She delivered her best work in the worst swamps I could find, so we became lowland specialists, pursuers of the web-footed rooster. We learned that skittish cocks are more likely to sit for a close flush in a swamp than elsewhere because they trust that heavy cover to hide them. In time I came to love marshes for their own sake. There is something wonderfully fundamental, stinky, and primal about a swamp. When I hold my nose against a rooster's body and inhale, he smells spicy and funky, like a marsh. Marshes smell like roosters to my dogs.

The second basic guideline for finding roosters derives from that classic principle of wildlife behavior, the "edge effect." Wildlife concentrates where two habitat types come together. It amuses me to think of such edges as seams where two sheets of habitat butt against each other. My dog and I run those seams like the busy needle of a sewing machine.

The top priority of a fall rooster is to eat without being eaten. So his daily activities center on little commutes between secure weeds and food, usually some grain crop. The seams along weeds and grain crops thus see more pheasant traffic than any other spot in the landscape. Look for roosters just inside the thick cover on the edge nearest food.

As the season moves along, finding pheasants becomes trickier because pheasants learn to stay away from the places where people with guns seek them. Roosters learn some crazy hunters will follow them into the most hellish cover, so they often alter strategies by frequenting light or oddball cover. They might loaf in isolated bits of brush along fences, in junk piles near the center of a section, or in the cottonwoods surrounding abandoned country schools. Pheasants learn which farms never allow hunting and become as canny about using them as any refuge-wise goose. They simply go where hunters don't go.

For that reason, by mid-season the roosters have been chased off most public hunting areas. Hunt private land then, especially farms with cover that cannot be seen from the road and farms that are selective about whom they welcome.

So a third plan for finding pheasants is to hunt where other people don't hunt. This slightly desperate strategy might direct you to bypass obviously attractive cover in favor of places that really shouldn't hold birds. Another classic pheasant hunting dilemma!

Your problems are not even half over when you find a rooster. The pheasant hunter's second basic skill is the ability to maneuver a cock into flushing in range. Like catching a greased pig, that's easier said than done.

Pheasant hunting is a moving game. You come at the birds. They counter by sliding away, trying to protect their thresholds of security. Moves and countermoves continue until something disrupts the pattern. The bird might skulk. He might run or flush wildly. If he can, he will veer left or right to flank you. Your goal is to push him into a place where he has nowhere to go but up.

Pheasants are often hunted by driving them with several hunters walking in a line. Drives are especially important for dogless hunters, as the width of the driving line makes it more difficult for pheasants to outflank hunters. In effect, drivers herd an imaginary flock of birds. They try to push that imaginary flock into a spot with no escape routes, pinning them against another line of hunters or against the limits of the cover. Then they learn if the flock is imaginary or real. Since pheasants often defeat drives by erupting out the far end of the cover, drives on experienced pheasants require blockers to plug that tempting exit.

Pheasants flush when—and usually *only* when—you deprive them of all other escape alternatives. They sneak until the cover peters out and further sneaking would expose them in all their multi-colored glory. Then they skulk or flush. If you are lucky, they delay flushing until you are in range.

Even with several accomplices, you cannot exert total control over the birds. Do what you will, it is difficult to trap roosters where they have no better option than to flush near you. You cannot force the birds to bend to your will.

Dogs change the game radically. No longer do you drive hypothetical flocks of birds, for dogs tell you whether birds are nearby or not. No longer can a rooster beat your drive by skulking. In fact, skulking is precisely what you want him to do, for it lets you get within range. A bird that sneaks or gets cute is no match for a good dog. Dogs can even get points or flushes on some running roosters.

But don't underestimate pheasants. Even hunters with dogs can't force roosters to flush in gun range. It is hard to deal with cocks that run without hesitating, and those pheasants that scramble into the skies at the distant sight of a hunter are unapproachable. Yet dogs vastly improve your chances of maintaining contact with moving birds and working them into boxes that have no easy exits.

You maneuver for flushes by using dogs, hunters, and the limitations of the cover to trap roosters in places where they'll skulk long enough for you to get in range. Then you intrude upon their circle of fear and await the result with a wildly racing heart.

*   *   *

There should be no excuse for missing this target. A three-pound rooster is about as large in the air as a kite. Because of a low wing-to-weight ratio, cocks labor for speed on the takeoff. A flushing rooster often calls attention to himself with brazen cackling. As if he weren't already as conspicuous as a Roman candle.

Obviously, those facts prove the pheasant is a target no wing-shot should miss. Ever.

Yet I have managed to do it and will again. The most times I've missed one rooster is five, and I only quit then because that was all the shells my gun held. Some birds I've missed were out of range, yet I recall with particular anguish those misses on birds flushing so close I felt their wing wind on my face.

A friend once burned up three boxes of shells to bag one rooster. To put it mildly, he found that frustrating. Just into his fourth box he missed another rooster at eight paces. Uttering a sulphurous oath, he whipped his expensive cowboy hat into the sky and touched off a shot. And wouldn't you know, he *shredded* the hat, which was a tougher shot than any of those roosters that got away. Even gifted wingshots miss. Bill Gallea once went thirteen for fourteen on ruffed grouse flushing in heavy cover, which as an act of athleticism ranks somewhere near running a three-minute mile. Two weeks later, that same athlete stood on a sunny Minnesota hillside with an empty gun, speaking in tongues while a jumbo rooster flapped away with only his pride hurt.

Pheasants must not be entirely easy to hit.

And they aren't. Anybody who sneers at pheasants as "easy" targets betrays the ignorance of a shooting preserve hotshot. A pheasant in a stiff breeze is the fastest target an upland hunter confronts. When a rooster hits his top speed while flying in a whooping prairie wind, I defy anyone to lead him by too much.

Past the opener, you get shots of all sorts, many tricky. Birds go up at greater ranges, on the back sides of trees or behind gauzy screens of cane. Often your footing is insecure. Timber roosters corkscrew through brush as erratically as any ruffed grouse. Late in the year when a cock flushes forty yards out, pounding low and hard and straight away, hitting him solidly is anything but easy.

Many people miss because of all that tail. Half a rooster's length is tail, and you must ignore it when you shoot. If you can do that you must still remember that only the front half of the body itself is a clean-kill zone. Shooting at the whole bird produces cripples, time and again. Whenever I expect a flush I remind myself my target is not the pheasant but his white neck ring.

Missing has a psychological component. Though pheasants are deemed slow, I've never seen anyone shoot in front of one. Flight speed, ultimately, is irrelevant. If roosters flew twice as fast or half as fast as they do, people would go right on shooting behind them . . . and by precisely the same distance. How can hunters miss such a big, gaudy, noisy target? They miss *because* that target is so big, gaudy, and noisy.

Me too. I wouldn't have it any other way.

TOM'S DREAM TRIP

— • 9 • —

I've never hunted with a more good-hearted man than Tom Huggler. Tom lives in Michigan where pheasants are even scarcer than in Minnesota. His enthusiasm for them might be all the greater for that.

Tom once invited me to join a South Dakota dream hunt he'd planned. We'd be hunting prime pheasant country in a year of bountiful bird populations. We would take our meals in the home of a farm host who would line up cover for us to work. All this would cost more than Tom and I were used to paying, but dream trips aren't supposed to be cheap.

Nothing, it would seem, could go wrong.

Nothing, except:

• Just before boarding his plane to South Dakota, Tom realized his dog lacked flying papers. He dashed in to check his baggage while his wife sped away on howling tires to the nearest vet. She returned seconds before the flight took off, in tears of tension.

• The flight turned out to be one of those toad-hopping operations that takes off and lands every fifteen minutes. Tom's setter was confined in an unheated cargo hold without water for most of a day. Tom fretted about her so much he was a bundle of nerves when he landed in South Dakota.

• Upon landing, Tom found his rental car was a rusty hunk of Detroit iron with no shocks and a motor that hammered like a woodpecker.

I met Tom at that point.

Brandy and I had driven across Minnesota, stopping to hunt some South Dakota public hunting areas late in the afternoon. While getting my station wagon gassed up I asked for advice on a place to hunt. The station owner was proud of an eight-point buck he'd just shot with his bow. "Got him while he was on top of a doe. Guess he died happy."

When someone at the gas station told me there was an area nearby where the weeds were so horrible even dogs couldn't root out the roosters, that's where we went. Brandy ran down two cocks in the swamp, putting them in the air right in front of me. Then she grabbed our third bird, a cripple, all on her own. I shucked my boots and pulled on a pair of mukluks, wiggling my toes in decadent comfort while the sun set under a smear of wispy clouds that bespoke a change of weather.

Then we met Tom. He was rattled by his flight but eager to take the most optimistic outlook on the dream hunt. We spent the night in a motel, leaving at dawn for the two-hour drive to the farm where we'd begin hunting. Tom said, "Well, it's been ragged so far, but I think the bad times are over with."

They were, except:

• As we packed, Tom put his never-worn $100 L. L. Bean hunting coat on top of the car and drove off with it up there. He remembered it forty highway miles later. Though we drove back all the way to the motel, we never saw the coat again. Tom had to hunt in a tiny orange vest that offered no warmth and a game bag barely big enough for two woodcock.

• Just as we started our first hunt, a blizzard struck. Temperatures dropped to Arctic levels, and the sky filled with pelting snow. Shrieking winds buffeted us and jangled the nerves of the pheasants.

• Tom's first shot of the trip crippled a cock that got away because

• his dog freaked out in the presence of all that bird scent and ran away,

• so Tom spent the first hour of the trip driving gravel roads looking for his lost dog. He found her in a field of milo where we had been strictly forbidden to hunt, but Tom had to reclaim his dog, so he went in and

• got his butt chewed by a red-faced farmer who assumed Tom had sashayed in where he knew he did not belong. So Tom and I went to a marsh where

• Tom learned his new hunting boots didn't fit, and he got horrible blisters that burned like glowing coals with every step he took. Then

• his second shot of the trip came on a perfect chance for a double, with two roosters up in the air just feet apart, fifteen yards away. Tom's eyes flitted from one cock to the other and then he poured five shots into the air between the birds,

• which caused his dog to take off again. So Tom had to run her down (each step hurting more than the last) and lock her in the car for the rest of the trip. Indeed, Tom saw that she would never hunt under control and so he'd have to get rid of her somehow and then buy and train another dog.

Understand, all this took place in the space of less than twenty-four hours. When did a dream ever unravel so quickly and disastrously?

At that point we split up. Brandy and I punched it hard. I popped one little rooster she trapped in a marsh. In the same marsh I missed two cocks that got into the gale and flashed by me faster than human arms could move a gun. Brandy then picked up a lively cripple she found in a creekbed. I finally scratched down our limit-out bird at day's end with a Hail Mary shot on a towering rooster some other hunters had kicked out of a distant cornfield.

I retreated to the car, poured coffee, lit a cigar, and shivered until the heater thawed my core. Then I went looking for Tom, as it was almost the end of shooting hours.

I found him near the forbidden milo field, and what a pathetic sight he was in the grim light of that dusk, limping around the outer edge of the field like an old man, leaning into the wind, wearing that dumb little vest. Sheets of snow whipped past his shoulders. From time to time Tom broke into little dashes that must have popped blisters.

When he finally tottered up to the car I said, "Tom, if you were a horse I'd shoot you to put you out of your misery. It's time to stop this insanity! Come out of the cold. Let's go pour twelve fingers of Scotch and try to put this in perspective."

Tom said, "Gee, there's ten minutes of shooting time left, and I'd like to hunt it out. I know I can't go in the milo, but I've found that if I walk around the edge and run every now and then I confuse a few birds. I got two roosters doing that. If you don't mind waiting, I'll hang in there until the day is done." And off he went.

I later learned that one of Tom's roosters fell in the milo. Tom laid his gun down before walking in to retrieve it because he didn't want to seem to be hunting where he wasn't welcome. He flushed two roosters on the way in.

Tom finally limped back to the car, shivering uncontrollably. His hair was full of snow.

He got to the car, let out a protracted sigh, and said, "Well, it's been a little rough so far, but I think the bad times are over. From here on out I believe we're going to have a helluva hunt!"

And, folks, we did.

ON SIOUX LAND

•───── 10 ─────•

As he left the office for his first South Dakota pheasant hunt, Jerry Hoffnagle swept his hat off and delivered a stirring speech. "I'm off to defend the Midwest from encroaching hordes of the Heathen Chinee! We are being invaded, overwhelmed! Hordes of Chinese pheasants threaten to cover every inch of the landscape. The western front is in South Dakota, where I and my gun are posted for duty. Sleep in peace, dear ones, for Jerry stands between you and all those roosters. Awayyy!"

The secretaries didn't look up. They already believed Jerry was one or two bubbles off plumb.

Bird numbers were spectacular that fall when we first hunted Sioux tribal land in the Missouri Breaks region. Jerry had recently come from Pennsylvania to manage sales for the small book publishing firm where Kathe was managing editor. We three became friends and planned a trip to show Jerry some Sioux ringnecks.

Jerry's Pennsylvania pheasant hunting had mostly involved crawling through bramble patches, leaving patches of skin to mark his back trail. With luck, a day of painful effort would produce shots on a rooster or two. Nothing in Jerry's background prepared him for his first sight of Missouri Breaks pheasant cover.

We stopped on a bluff overlooking a grand sweep of grass stretching unbroken for miles in two directions. Above the grass was a milo field. Beyond the grass the mighty Missouri pitched uneasily in a stiff wind. Chatty Jerry went silent. He said with awe, "There's more cover in front of me right now than exists in all of Pennsylvania. Where are the bramble patches? Where are the little spots with birds? This is going to be like hunting on Mars!"

We combed that Martian grass for an hour, finding only one rooster. Brandy ran him down in the weedy fringe of the milo field. Apparently every other pheasant in that corner of the reservation was in the crops where we weren't allowed to go. So we moved. Soon our red Fairmont was parked along the long ribbon of cover we came to call "The Golf Course."

Here there was no milo, just miles of prairie grass, pocket marshes, old shelterbelts, juniper groves, buckbrush clumps, plum thickets, and patches of kochia. Brushy draws snaked down to join the Missouri River, terminating in mucky deltas where cattails flourished.

We uncased guns and examined the cover to make a plan. Too late. Brandy wasn't going to wait for a plan when she had a snoot full of scent. I'd just closed the action on my SKB when her rooster hammered low and fast out of the junipers.

The next hour was a pheasant hunting clinic conducted by a nine-year-old springer. I had expected this to be the year Brandy went into her old age decline. Instead it was the first of the five best years she gave me. Brandy slashed and cruised and bounced until we had eight beautiful roosters. Kathe said "Brinka is a good hunter, but Brandy's the dog that gets things started." It was an observation so accurate I always afterward thought of it as the most appropriate epitaph for her.

As we began the drive down a draw for our last bird, I was subliminally aware of an odd sound we'd been hearing all afternoon. The sound seemed out of place, although that was more of a feeling than a thought. Brandy and Brinka crisscrossed each other chasing scent near the river. Two hens broke out to my left, then a rooster hooked to the right, toward Kathe. Jerry hailed Kathe's good shot.

Then we fell silent.

We walked the final steps toward the river and the strange sound. The wind had whipped the water into a surf—not waves, but a true ocean surf that boomed rhythmically on the shore. After slaking their thirst in the river, the dogs lounged on elbows to pant in bliss and let the wind make flags of their ears. We sat there without speaking while the sweat on our brows became chalky salt. Breakers thudded against the beach, throwing a rainbowed spray over the roosters lovingly laid out on the sand. Out in front of us immense rafts of geese rode the unquiet waves.

Back at the motel, Jerry and I cleaned birds on a picnic bench and toasted the day with glasses of peaty whiskey. The surface of the big river, wrinkled like pudding, mirrored the evening sky as it slid past blue hills on its way toward Nebraska. I've never understood why western sunsets are so spectacular, but they are. This one was as subtle as an old Wurlitzer jukebox. Plum and cerise dollops of cloud, bordered in hot platinum, floated in a coral sky while shafts of sunlight radiated like searchlights through cloud cracks. The sky was holding nothing back.

Jerry sighed. "Ah, life is real, life is earnest! I've never been so happy. This is perfection. Beautiful country, great dog work, a limit of birds, then Scotches under a Technicolor sunset. This is the absolute definition of happiness."

"No, no," I protested. "Happiness is a relative, not an absolute, condition. If we'd come expecting to shoot fifteen birds, we'd be disappointed with nine. Happiness is what you feel when things go better than you thought they would."

"Wrong! Wrong!" Jerry howled. "This *is* happiness. You couldn't have a day like this without being ultimately happy. Every possible condition for absolute happiness has been met!"

Kathe came by, shaking her head in disgust. "I can't believe you guys. You're talking profound bullshit. It was a great day."

She was right, of course.

Every now and then—and it sure isn't often—you blunder into a situation where the hunting is too easy. You don't entertain such thoughts at the time, when your blood is rushing and you are cresting on the high all predators must feel after a kill. Ah, but later . . . later the niggling voice of conscience pipes up with its uncomfortable questions. I don't know about yours, but my conscience has a high, fussy tone, somewhere between an aging male librarian and Jiminy Cricket.

"Really, I say, really! Wasn't that too much of a sure thing? The birds didn't have a chance!"

That's how it was on the second day we hunted The Golf Course. An east wind whooped all day, causing tears to well in our eyes and our clothes to flap like storm pennants. Wind usually makes pheasants paranoid and unapproachable. Once in a blue moon, though, it works for the hunter.

If we walked into the wind, toward the river, the pheasants couldn't hear us until we were close enough to shake salt on their tails. When the birds moved away from us they ended up in the wet weedy draw ends where they might find temporary safety. But only temporary, for they had laid a scent trail that Brandy and Brinka traced with busy noses.

At the river, the birds faced a rock-and-hard-place decision. To take advantage of the wind they would have to flush and peel back toward our guns. If they went straight away from us they would be trying to fly into that torrent of wind.

We finished that day in a short draw that ended in a riverside patch of cattails, bulrushes, and prairie sand reed. Brandy and Brinka cruised the cover with joy, Brinka's tail lashing expressively, Brandy's stub buzzing like a tuning fork. There were birds ahead of us. In fact, there was a whole flock. The dogs said so. We closed the trap, surrounding the clump, while tension increased like a guitar string tightened up to the breaking point. The rushes began to rattle with wings. Dogs careened through the cattails, trying to snag birds as they went up. We could hear the raspy cackling of roosters over the din of the wind.

A small cock jumped in front of me and tried to hack a path up the wind. I held fire until I couldn't stand it any longer, then pitched the gun up and shot . . . still much too close. Kathe's and Jerry's guns boomed amidst cries of "Hen—don't shoot!" and *"Rooster, rooster, rooster!"*

Birds spiraled out of the waving cattails left and right. A hen surged up, banked low, and almost took my hat off as she rocketed by. Then an old cock broke on the far side of the patch, got out over the water and hooked to pass me with the full might of the wind in his wings. He crossed with the velocity of a highballing bluebill. When I cracked the trigger he smacked three times on the river like a skipping stone.

It wasn't until later that I considered feeling guilty. Conscience began examining my conduct like a dentist probing with a pick.

"Hold on, bearded boy, I've got a major beef with you. Wasn't that just too sweet a setup? I mean, really, did the birds have a chance?"

Oh, for Maud's sake, Conscience! You are such a blue-nosed

prig! Yes, we had them in a box today. But where were you those two bitter days down by Baxter when my eyelashes kept freezing together? Where were you that time when the honeysuckle thorns had me snagged by the tender flesh of my groin while the damned birds were running circles around me? Or that day in the rain. Ha, *Ha*! Remember the day in the rain when I had pneumonia and the cover was as cold as a corpse and I got those huge balls of gumbo on my boots? Remember that? I didn't hear a peep from you then, you crummy phony summertime soldier! *BUZZ OFF!*

In the next days, Jerry sent dozens of postcards to friends and family back East to say that, after this hunt, Heaven was going to be a letdown. His favorite was a comic card showing a hunter asleep on the ground, slumped against a fencepost. A rooster (obviously stuffed) stands before him, staring quizzically. There is a huge question mark over the rooster's head.

On our fourth day we were driving out for a new set of Golf Course adventures when I experienced a domestic emergency. It was one of those times when Nature calls—on the Hot Line. I had to find a bush, and quick. I whipped the car into a skidding turn down a side road and sprinted behind a plum thicket with toilet paper.

When I came back out, I couldn't believe my eyes. More than a dozen pheasants strolled around the car. A hen pecked gravel next to one of the Ford's tires. Roosters struck regal poses, their heads gleaming in the sun. I sucked in my breath and watched with unbearable anticipation. At any moment the car doors would explode outward. Dogs would bolt at the birds while hunters fumbled shells into their guns. Whooeee, this would be something to see!

But nothing happened. Nothing kept happening. What were they waiting for?

The Ford's windshield reflected the dappled sky like a mirror. Then a cloud shuttered the sun and I could see. Brandy and Brinka were curled as tight as hedgehogs in the back, dead asleep. Jerry and Kathe sat slumped in the front seats with heads tipped against the head rests, sleeping the sleep of the anesthetized.

A haughty rooster glowered at our crimson car, trying to remember if it had been here the last time he came this way. He drew himself up at full length until it seemed he was looking down on the Ford. I could see the big question mark over his head.

We returned to that land every fall for several years. Pheasants were never again as abundant as that first year, though we had many superb hunts on land we increasingly came to love. In time that land acquired additional appeals as memories accumulated like layers of hand-rubbed oil on a highly figured stock.

Not all the memories were pleasant.

It often felt odd to pursue pleasure within sight of Indian families living in poverty. We occasionally felt the guilt of sybaritic aristocrats seeking amusement who are unexpectedly exposed to the mean lives of an underclass.

Though we sought to be exquisitely polite, now and then we managed to infuriate Indian landowners. We had conflicts that were disturbing, one or two that were frightening.

Our relations with Indians were especially scratchy the year we hunted with The Odd Couple. Sandy and Tyler, hunters from Indiana staying at our motel, were a study in opposites. Sandy was nervous, compulsively neat, and obsessed with keeping his mint-new Cherokee free of scratches. Each time after parking it, Sandy scurried about covering the Cherokee with magnetic-backed foam bumpers. Tyler, who had inherited all the natural athletic ability that Sandy had been shorted, was as relaxed as a plate of linguine.

We met in the motel parking lot one day after hunting. They were disconsolate about their poor hunting, staring as we cleaned nine roosters. We agreed to take them with us on Sioux land the next day to show them a better time. I don't remember much about the hunting except that Sandy, in the way of so many American males, was furiously keeping score in some kind of competitive game only he was playing.

At one point Tyler and I had to use a gravel road to get back to the car. "Better unload your gun, Tyler," I said, "because they've got a law about that and the current game warden is a guy who purely hates whites. He'd love any excuse to fine our pink butts." We walked along in awkward silence for several minutes. I finally added lamely, "Uhhh, I don't know how he feels about fining black butts." For Tyler was no whiter than Bill Cosby. In my anxiety about Indians I had made Tyler an honorary Caucasian.

One year I learned a new definition of heartache. Birds were down that year because a spring hailstorm had shattered eggs and pummeled pheasant chicks. The prairie was strewn with the debris of young pheasant life that was never to be.

Yet there were highlights.

Brinka, rebounding from hip dysplasia surgery, hunted with more zest and sense of purpose than she had ever before shown. She made a thrilling swimming retrieve on a cripple that fell in a flooded patch of willows. We could only hear what happened. Brinka churned around in there so many minutes I guessed the rooster was diving like a duck. Brinka wouldn't give up. We stood outside the willows listening to her puffing and stroking. Then puffing turned to snorting because Brinka had a mouthful of rooster and was breathing through her nose. We all cheered her gritty effort.

The best retrieve of her life was to be her last.

A day later we walked back to the car, dusty and exhausted. As Brinka passed me, I heard bare bone grinding on bare bone. Years of running with bad hips had destroyed the cartilage in her knees. In that moment I knew Brinka would never take another step as a hunter. In the next moment I knew we would have to give her away, as we couldn't afford to keep a non-hunting dog in our home. Ah Brinka, sweet Brinka! Why did this have to happen to the one we loved so well?

What is heartache? Heartache is locking a dog in the car and walking away while she howls in disbelief at being abandoned; hearing her moaning when you are a mile off in the prairie; trying unsuccessfully to think about hunting while your wife walks through the undulating grass, her cheeks glistening with silent tears.

A THINKING MAN'S GAME

• 11 •

Pheasant hunting is as simple as sex. You throw a dog in the weeds and follow him with a gun. Tiddleywinks is more complicated.

Pheasant hunting is as complicated as sex. Attempting to find and outmaneuver roosters is a daunting enterprise that can't be recommended to people who take themselves too seriously. Pheasant hunting is a thinking man's game, more arcane and complicated than chess.

Then again, you can make pheasant hunting as simple or complex as you choose. The second man who taught me pheasant hunting loved it as a brainless, physical game. Gary called his gonzo hunting style "a train wreck in a swamp." On the other hand, I am an analytical person who cannot quit asking,

"Am I doing a dumb thing?" Since I can't turn off my brain, I try to enjoy it. I'm forever trying to impose patterns of logic on the chaos of experience.

The higher levels of pheasant hunting have nothing to do with bag limits and everything to do with understanding pheasants. The advanced hunter tries to think like a rooster, tries to predict where birds will be and how they will behave. Don't expect perfection. If you're right three times in ten, you're batting for a higher average than many millionaire baseball players. The intricacies of the mental game enhance a sport already rich in aesthetic appeal and physical challenges.

I struggled to understand pheasants until I grasped the enormity of the effects of pressure. Until you know how much experience pheasants in an area have had with human hunters, you cannot predict them. Virtually every statement you have heard about pheasants is both true and untrue: true for some birds and untrue for others. Pressure makes the difference.

Do pheasants have a daily routine, moving at predictable times to predictable locations? Sure they do—until the opening day of the season. Then they make startling changes that follow no predictable pattern except you can be sure the new behavior of the birds will be calculated to frustrate your intentions as a hunter.

Is it true that pheasants sit for close flushes in the dense weeds of marshes? Yes, indeed. Many do, especially birds that have successfully eluded predators before by wriggling into marshy pockets. Other pheasants will sprint through swamps at speeds you wouldn't think possible on a sloppy track. Such birds have learned rude lessons about swamp-busting Labradors.

Do smart roosters beat hunters by skulking? Some do, some don't. Skulking is the natural way a young bird in cover escapes detection. If you hunt land that has been worked lightly by town boys and a weekend hunter or two, expect to find skulkers. But in cover that has been vacuumed repeatedly by springers and shorthairs, any remaining roosters will have a poor opinion of skulking.

You see the pattern.

Several clues tip you to the fact that an area has been hunted hard. You don't want to see piles of bird feathers where hunters park their cars. You don't want to see shiny shell hulls in the grass. An even more discouraging sign is heavy cover that has hunter highways stomped through it.

You can't conclude much either way from the fact that you are not seeing roosters. They could just be elsewhere. A high hen-to-rooster ratio is a bad sign, although not conclusive proof of heavy pressure. Late in the season, roosters often hang out together away from the hens. If you haven't found them, you still might.

The most reliable evidence of hunter pressure is bird behavior. Now and then you'll get on the trail of a bird that runs like a gazelle before erupting into flight far ahead. If that bird is a cock, he's behaving like an experienced rooster. You'll need persistence and skill to bag pheasants in this place. I hope your legs are strong and your dog knows his game. Ah, but if that bird is a hen, you have my condolences. Pressure has been vociferous on this land. The smart way to hunt such areas is to go somewhere else as rapidly as possible.

One of the most disheartening sights I know is birds flushing out of range and flying a short distance before dropping back into the cover. Such short-hop flights in heavy cover are the hallmark of battlewise birds that know hunters but also know they are in perfectly secure cover.

Kathe, Jerry, and I once bucked through a South Dakota marsh whose towering cattails shut out the sun. From time to time, Tess and Brandy had scent but lost it. The dogs seemed to be trying to work a mobile flock of birds. Then a pair of hens went up well over two hundred yards ahead of us, flying until they pitched back in the marsh on the fringes of our vision. "Uh, oh!" I groaned. "Bye, bye marsh. We're outta here!"

There was no point going on. We had found a flock of pheasants so jangled by pressure they wouldn't let humans anywhere near them. In the most secure weeds imaginable, their threshold of anxiety had a radius of a quarter of a mile. Even if we'd had Robert E. Lee plotting strategy for us, we were never going to be a threat to those birds.

Sometimes the only pattern is that there is no pattern. Randomly scattered pheasants result from the chaos of opening day crowds. At such times you just grind out the miles until you cut fresh scent.

But most days there is a pattern. Roosters and hens might be in different types of cover, yet most roosters will use the same type of cover at a given time of day. If you find one cock you can often find others by duplicating the pattern.

The largest cattail marsh Brandy and I ever hunted was South Dakota's Lake Preston. In dry years, Preston is known oxymoronically as a "dry lake," meaning it is thirty-three thousand acres of marsh weeds. Brandy and I could have roamed those weeds for a week without working the same spot twice. There had to be a smarter plan. Roosters were probably concentrated in small areas. But where?

I began my search by eliminating areas of the marsh where the adjacent cornfields were unharvested. We hunted, instead, parts of the marsh lying next to cut corn. I also ruled out the heart of the marsh because I assumed a rooster in the second week of the season wouldn't trouble himself to fly so far after loading his crop with corn.

Brandy and I spent half an hour checking the outer edge of cattails near harvested fields. In our years together we found hundreds of roosters by stitching such seams. But not this day.

Apparently there had been enough hunting pressure to force the birds off the edges.

We moved about a quarter of a mile deeper into the marsh. There my eye was drawn to a tall patch of phragmites. The phragmites offered the only cover variety in a jillion acres of cattails. Brandy popped inside the cane patch, reappearing inches behind the tail of a rooster.

Aha!

While Brandy retrieved the first bird, I spotted several other stands of phragmites a quarter of a mile in from cut corn. We sauntered up to two more, and a rooster blasted out of each one. After nailing down the pattern, it was a short hunt.

If pheasant hunting were that formulaic it would lose its challenge and appeal. Fret not, dear reader! The Red Gods feed us these moments of triumph to set us up for ultimate humiliations. We all know what pride goeth before. Still, it is pleasant now and then to believe you understand how you won a quick limit, fun to be "sure" the next patch of phragmites would have held another rooster.

Luckily, I didn't have to find out.

To hunt is to pursue, and that also means you move. Or so it is with pheasant hunting. The sport has a dynamism, a flow, that is more like hockey than baseball. You move.

Many hunts proceed like a downhill ski run, with a hurtling momentum punctuated by countless little decisions. Should you slow it down or pick up the speed? Turn or go ahead? Should you do these knapweeds upwind or catch them on the downwind sally? Are those sidehill Russian olives worth working systematically, or can you give them a lick and a promise? Most of these decisions take place somewhere in the back of the brain where you aren't aware of them but where you can, if need be, drag them forward into the light for conscious scrutiny.

Pheasant hunting also resembles chess. Pheasant hunting and chess unfold as a series of moves and countermoves. You think: "If I do this, how will the rooster counter?" Just as in chess, you try to think a move or two ahead. You must, for the roosters surely do.

Unlike chess, the game board in pheasant hunting—the cover—keeps changing as you pass through it. As the shape and texture and size of the cover alters, the possibilities it offers for pursuit and evasion shift constantly.

At one moment the cover might lie like a river of weeds that only allows pheasants to move upriver as you come at them. Later that river might acquire tributaries, weedy spurs that converge with the main course. Each tributary poses questions, complications, opportunities. Do you break off your thrust on the main channel to check out each side course? Some days you should; some days you shouldn't. You make these decisions on the fly.

Meanwhile, your mind zooms in and out to take macro or microscopic views of the hunt. At the micro level, you are the center of a sphere of influence about forty yards wide. This smallest circle is the only one beginning hunters can perceive. Even an expert hunter moving in difficult terrain has to bring his concentration down to this tight circle.

Beyond that there is a greater sphere of influence that encompasses you, all your partners, and all of the dogs. As you walk along you consider what is happening on the borders of this larger area. I believe good hunters have their minds focused most often at this level of generality.

Experienced hunters can expand to a more comprehensive field of awareness, something like a camera lens that can zoom back to extreme wide angle perspectives. This larger field of perception encompasses the overall layout of the cover and its many elements, including those lying out of sight.

Remember that this superior level of awareness is always available to the pheasant. You are on his home ground. To emulate the pheasant's perception of the landscape a hunter has to imagine he is in the sky—as a pheasant has often been—looking down upon the mosaic of all habitat components in the area.

I recall the day I first grasped this macroscopic view of habitat. Brandy and I had worked a delicious weedy draw in a field of cut corn in Iowa without finding even a wisp of scent. I was upset. I thought, "Aarrgh! I'll never understand these birds! This place has everything they need. Why aren't they here?"

Then I glanced at the neighbor's field, lying just across a little valley. It had both cut and uncut corn. It had more draws, with thicker weeds than those Brandy had just swept. And the whole works was surrounded by *No Trespassing* signs. Birds weren't "here" because there was more of what they needed "there," just twenty wingbeats and a glide away.

As you walk cover, try to visualize the overall pattern of the land as a pheasant knows it. In time you will see that pheasants never flush in random directions. They always go to some definite place, which will be the most secure spot they know in the immediate area. If you follow them you may gain a second or third flush. You sometimes find a new spot to hunt. Better, you gain insights into the logic of their moves.

I once kicked up a pheasant from some Minnesota alders on a drizzly November afternoon. As the bird disappeared in the misty pewter sky, nothing about it said "rooster" loud enough to permit me to shoot. Just my luck: the only pheasant I'd seen all day was a UFO. But I thought I knew where he was going, if "he" was a he. Half an hour earlier, Brandy had snuffled through a triangle of dense weeds abutting a field of standing corn. Though Brandy said there was no scent there, I had noted the spot as the most promising bit of cover in the whole area.

We backtracked to the weedy triangle, Brandy on heel. Because I expected the bird to break toward the corn, the other secure cover in the area, I stood between the corn and the weed patch before releasing Brandy. Within seconds the bird was in the air, very much a rooster, flying toward the corn.

Older men—one might prefer to say *seasoned* men—learn to substitute quality for quantity. I once had the dream of hunting pheasants every day for a solid month. Until someone pays me to hunt pheasants, my longest string will remain twenty-four days short of that. So be it. Instead, I dream these days of putting together the perfect hunt.

A perfect hunt would only be possible in some vast heath with exceptional cover diversity, a great woolly wasteland of impossible weeds with a sign overhead to tell hunters, "Abandon hope, all ye who enter here." It would have raunchy fens and windswept uplands and an erratic array of weedy draws connecting them to a loopy little creek bottom. Tucked away in obscure corners of the area would be subtle little cover clumps, and I'd want a few huge willow patches shaped like Rorschach blots.

We'd need a few roosters in those weeds. Just a few. Give us educated but still huntable cocks. An ideal hunt would feature pheasants that have outmaneuvered men and dogs often enough to make them confident of doing it again.

The perfect hunt would develop like a musical composition whose diverse movements are reconciled to the whole through subtle internal logic. Spook and I would shift from *allegro con brio* to *andante* as the occasion required. We would mix time-proven tactics with inspired bold strokes. We would move intuitively without knowing which way we were going next, yet we would know what the roosters were going to do before they themselves knew.

I cannot picture the specifics of this hunt. All I know with certainty is how it would feel, for I have experienced a few moments of perfect hunting. At such moments I feel . . . oh, words are such impotent, clumsy things at times! At such moments all conscious thought and all the trappings of civilization drop away from me until I—a sentimental, self-conscious guy—feel as naked and keenly focused as a needle. I become a pure predator with total confidence in my body and a shocking commitment to kill. And it is heady, heady, heady.

I imagine falcons routinely feel what I have felt for a few scorchingly intense moments. If so, they are to be envied. And what a coy twist this is: the ultimate objective of the thinking man's approach to this sport is to transcend all thought to become, if briefly, just another of God's bloody, innocent predators.

SCHEME, SCHEME, SCHEME!

• 12 •

I was a child of four when I found the robin's nest in our front yard. The bird had interlaced grass and twigs with cunning to create a structure as light as it was strong. I was impressed. "Gee," I thought, "if a dumb little bird can make something as nifty as this, just *imagine* what I and my big brain could do!" I collected grass and twigs. Then I sat under a hollyhock trellis and began to weave my nest. Minutes later, chagrined, I threw the bird's exquisitely crafted nest and the pile of crud I'd made under the house where I wouldn't have to suffer the sight of them again.

It was the first time I was humiliated by a bird. It wasn't to be the last.

*   *   *

When we were penniless college students, Bill and I frequently drove to central Iowa for late-season pheasant hunts. A friend, Jim Layton, let us camp out in a drafty utility barn behind his house. The metal barn was chilly on a December night as we slept on the concrete floor in thin sleeping bags, but the price was right.

Our favorite farm was a lazily cultivated place tucked down in a serpentine river valley in southwestern Iowa. In a wet year, you got the impression the farmer expected a strong market for fall cockleburs and foxtail, for that's what he put most of the farm into, having planted a little corn as a backup if his weeds didn't fetch a good price. We called this farm The Rooster Factory because it produced so many birds.

There was a dandy bit of cover around a stock dam that sat at the conjunction of a weedy fenceline and a nasty draw filled with smartweed and horseweeds. That spot always held a flock of pheasants.

The first time we hunted The Rooster Factory we reached the stock dam by walking along the fenceline west to east. That was the logical, convenient way to go. Before we got in range, fifteen pheasants clattered out the east side. Humph! They'd seen hunters before.

That night in the utility barn we plotted a fresh assault on the stock dam pheasants. We agreed we'd gone wrong by doing the too-obvious thing. *Scheme, scheme, scheme!*

The next day we crossed the birds up, looping around to come at them from the east side. These birds apparently had seen that one too. They all went out the west end, dropping whitewash and giving us the Bronx cheer as they went.

We were really ready the third day. Bill and Jim sneaked along the fence from the west, while Brandy and I slipped noiselessly in from the east. That day the pheasants ran down the draw and flushed out the south end of the cover.

The strategy session in the utility barn was intense the next night. We drew maps with little arrows. *Scheme, scheme, scheme!* In the morning, Jim crept up the south draw, Bill sneaked across from the west, and Brandy and I tippy-toed in from the east. We moved in silence and timed our approach so we'd all hit the pond at once. Long before we were in range, the whole flock boiled out of the north side of the dam. They escaped from the only weeds we couldn't cover since they were across the fence on the neighbor's land.

Mercifully, that was the last day of our hunt. We were spared further humiliation from that pheasant coven.

I once briefly joined a gang of six hunters in central South Dakota, the last time I hunted with such an unwieldy party. We spent as much time bickering about tactics as we did hunting.

One afternoon we ran a little drive through a shelterbelt, being careful to post blockers first. But the drivers and blockers were nowhere near each other when a cock foiled our plan by flushing from the middle of the cover. According to our script, he was supposed to run toward the blockers and then panic and flush in their faces. He seemed to know all about blockers.

But he'd made a fatal mistake. We saw where he landed. The fenceline he flew to was surrounded by bare plowed fields with no escape cover. He was isolated in a patch of grass no bigger than a sofa.

Scheme, scheme, scheme!

After a windy strategy session, the gang again divided into two groups. Each squad walked a quarter of a mile to either side of the rooster's hiding spot, then rushed together along the fence. Oh ho! The old pincers maneuver!

Brandy and I sat on a hill to watch. I was ostensibly letting the other guys take the Sure Thing. Actually, I didn't care to get my pheasants in that kind of hunt. And I'd seen that rooster beat a perfectly organized drive. He didn't figure to be a bird stupid enough to enter a trap with no exit.

Five men and four dogs converged on the weed patch . . . which, of course, was empty. Don't ask me how. Maybe the rooster strolled away across the plowing while we plotted his demise.

In those years when Kathe, Jerry, and I hunted Sioux land in South Dakota, we always ran across a big cabal of pheasants in the same spot. Those birds drove me bonkers. They were almost impossible to hunt.

Their sanctuary was an island, maybe eight acres in size, which was separated from the mainland by eighty yards of Missouri River. Close to the island, but on shore, there was a formidable stand of bulrushes, sedges, phragmites, and cattails. Those weeds were no fun to hunt. They reached the height of a basketball hoop, and at their base lay a jumble of logs in a foot of water. To approach the island birds, we had to make a conspicuous descent down a long slope. By the time we got all the way down the hill, the roosters knew the size of our party, the breed of each dog, and which of us toted 12-gauges.

Years later, I learned that in the office that sold tribal hunting licenses, the Indian wildlife managers invariably directed hunters to that same piece of ground. "You're sure to see lots of pheasants there," they'd say. By the time we got around to hunting that area, those pheasants had outwitted humans a hundred times or so. We didn't know that. We just knew those birds were damned hard to approach.

Time after time, we'd descend that hill only to see sixty or seventy pheasants flushing wildly. Some went to the shoreline cattails. Most flew directly to the island. The birds had a few other escape routes, too, but they didn't need them. The cattail patch was secure cover and the island an unimpregnable castle surrounded by a moat. The Indian managers were uncommonly precise when they described that spot. It was a great place to *see* pheasants.

The island pheasants became a burr under my saddle. By this time I was representing myself in print as a pheasant expert, which can be a miserable cross to bear. *Scheme, scheme, scheme!*

By approaching the cattails via unusual routes, we enjoyed some minor triumphs. If we put our dogs on heel and released them after doing our best to surround the shoreline cattails, we bagged a cock now and then. Yet I kept thinking the man who had written a book about pheasant tactics should be able to pull off something more clever.

Then one year the rains fell mainly elsewhere than on the plains. The mighty Missouri shrank from its banks, and we saw the water between shore and the island was not overly deep. We could infiltrate the island sanctuary if we didn't mind getting wet. Jerry declared, "Revenge is ours! Behold, the Red Sea lies parted. Let's go for it!"

We sloshed out there in river water just over our boots, walking cautiously, dogs at heel, whispering so we wouldn't spook the birds off the island. Fat chance of that! That island grew the rankest, loftiest, nastiest weeds it has ever been my displeasure to enter. A man couldn't move in that rain forest without swinging a machete. As if the weeds weren't horrible enough, they masked a maze of driftwood that I kept banging with my shins. It was like hunting in an auto graveyard, blindfolded.

Brandy was ten then, with nearly all her youthful vigor. I would have bet my house that no piece of cover on earth could keep roosters safe from Brandy. I would have lost my house. Brandy bashed around desperately without result. I couldn't see her—heck, I couldn't see four feet ahead of my nose—but I tried to keep near the considerable ruckus she was making. Now and then a hen left the island. Three times roosters cursed Brandy as they flapped up to shoulder height and dropped back into the cover again almost immediately. They had so much confidence in those weeds they only moved enough to keep from being bitten. I could hear the pitter patter of pheasant feet as birds skittered around us. Brinka and Kathe were having the same luck, while dogless Jerry never stood a chance.

We spilled enormous amounts of human and canine energy on that island before beating a retreat back across the water, wet, sweaty, and utterly chastened.

Years later over beers in a bar in Pierre, two guides asked me, "You ever see that island out there on Indian land? The one with all the smart birds?" They, too, had been challenged by the mighty flock of visible but unhuntable roosters. There had to be a way. *Scheme, scheme, scheme!* They loaded three big walleye boats with hunters and Labradors. On a signal, boats zoomed in from three points of the compass. Dogs and hunters boiled out in a sort of Iwo Jima beachhead assault. Trying to keep a straight face, I asked what success they'd had. *"Never saw a bleeping bird!"*

Our best attack on the island birds was our last. Kathe, Jerry, and I synchronized watches and split up. Kathe and Tess sat below the crest of the hill, below the sightline of the pheasant lookouts. Meanwhile Jerry and I walked—quietly and bent at the waist for concealment—for half an hour until we were in position on the shoreline. Jerry was north of the island and the cattails; Pogo and I were south of them.

At the appointed time, Kathe and Tess began sauntering down the hill. They were our distraction. You will recognize this strategy's origin in Winnie the Pooh's famous balloon-assisted assault on the honey tree. Jerry and I took off running along the shoreline in a ferocious effort to get on the river side of the cattails before the pheasants flushed to the island. If we were quick enough, the cocks couldn't reach their refuge without flying over us.

Alas, we picked an unlucky year to try this. Usually the

shoreline was sandy and firm, but Jerry and I made our wild charges through about two feet of a substance aquatic biologists refer to as loonshit. Jerry impaled himself on some driftwood; I made it into the zone between the cattails and the island. Bird after bird sailed over my head on their way to the island, mostly out of range.

I think we got three roosters that day, which means some thirty cocks made safe exits. We also got thoroughly stinky, slimy, and wet. It was a tactical victory of a highly qualified sort. Give us credit for some sense. We knew better than to pull the same stunt on the same birds again.

This comes perilously close to Ed Zern's system for hunting crows. Zern's technique is based on the scientific fact that crows can't count past thirteen. The hunt is set up by having different sized groups of hunters in costumes running back and forth between two blinds. Nine guys rush to one blind wearing Richard Nixon masks, three put on false whiskers and run back, then four return wearing berets in different colors, et cetera. Meanwhile the crows in the trees are counting madly. Do this correctly, Zern promises, and you'll end up with one hunter in the blind whom the crows have lost track of.

Scheme, scheme, scheme!

If we ever take a shot at those island pheasants again, I know just what to do. We'll dress Kathe as an equestrienne. Then Jerry and I will get in one of those vaudeville horse suits. . .

A LAND SHAPED
BY WIND

—— • 13 • ——

The Missouri Breaks country in South Dakota lies in gentle folds like a rumpled carpet. Eons of prairie wind have smoothed out all rough places, leaving an undulating landscape with sensual contours. It is one of the enigmas of prairie that it seems so flat to your eyes but so vertical to your legs. As you walk this swelling, dipping land you might be reminded of sand dunes or mounds of ice milk, though I see thighs and bosoms.

Wind is the omnipresent force of prairie, scouring the land like a cornstalk broom. Some prairie grasses have skins reinforced with silica, making them rude versions of fiberglass fishing rods. Yet even these win their battle with the wind by yielding the main points and hanging on for dear life. To any organism asserting itself by standing upright, the wind says,

"Let's wrestle!" And because the wind never tires, it always wins. Prairie shrubs huddle discreetly in the lees of hollows and draws. Trees hide in river bottoms where the full might of wind cannot find them. King wind rules all.

The apparent desolation of prairie affects different people differently. I once hunted the nearby Nebraska Sandhills with an Iowan who turned suddenly cranky after a two-hour walk over draws so complicated we couldn't remain near each other. That night he apologized, explaining that he'd been terrified by the scale of his surroundings and had seen himself dying alone in that trackless waste, crawling toward an oasis mirage like a figure in a cartoon. In a lifetime of hunting Iowa he'd never been out of sight of something manmade.

The land is big, empty, and virtually unchanged from the way it looked to Lewis and Clarke in 1804. Lewis walked the very ground Kathe and I hunt, being astonished by the "immence herds of Buffaloe, deer Elk and Antelopes." Deer and antelope are still common, though the elk have been pushed into the mountains and the only buffalo we saw grazed placidly behind fences, waiting for the eastern sportsmen who pay a thousand dollars apiece to come "hunt" them.

Kathe and I first hunted the Missouri Breaks a decade ago, falling in love with its cornucopia of fauna. Jackrabbits sprinted to the horizon, ungainly animals that obviously needed lessons in proper running form, though we learned a jack has many throttle settings and can outdistance a bird dog with insouciant ease. Coyotes trotted out of buffaloberry clumps, looking vaguely annoyed. Mule deer pogo-sticked away from us, then stopped on distant crests to study us and present comical jug-eared profiles. Whitetails were down among riverbank willows, and two bolted by me so close I could have touched them. Because prairie is the natural domain of sight-hunters, raptors were everywhere; kestrels perched on phone poles, red-tailed hawks skirred overhead, and harriers floated like Frisbees just a few feet above the waving grass. Prairie dogs, when we drew near their housing developments, piped insults at us, popping in and out of view like vitriolic Jacks-in-the-box.

Overarching all was a haunting sound we had never heard before, a primitive gurgling coo that emanated from the skies with no apparent source. For two days Kathe and I puzzled over it before we realized we were hearing the fluting trills of sandhill cranes as they wheeled in sketchy Xs high above the prairie. The experience made a believer of me: birds *did* evolve from dinosaurs. Or so it seemed as we stood with heads tipped to watch the migrating families of feathered dragons that roamed the skies on mighty wings and called to us from somewhere deep in the Eocene.

We had splendid hunting that year on good numbers of birds that were almost too spooky to approach. Early-season hunters had educated the birds well. We would often top one ridge to see a flock of pheasants boiling off the crest of the next ridge, a pure picture of panic in feathered form.

As we approached one large wildlife area we were greeted by four roosters posing under the sign proclaiming this to be a public hunting area. There was no mistaking that invitation! Yet those pheasants flushed out of range twice, leaving us feeling we'd been conned. Kathe and I pushed deeper into open grassy prairie on the back side of the area where we hoped few other hunters had gone. There I wounded a cock that flushed at the sun. It was so hot, dry, and windy that Brandy's nose could pull no trace of scent from the bird. She demonstrated her accumulated bird savvy by running from spot to spot of the type a crippled pheasant crawls into. After minutes of methodical sight searching, Brandy thrust her head under some palmetto and came up with my rooster, as proud as Jack Horner.

We entered a great valley, Kathe and Brinka walking along an old river bed, Brandy and I scaling the bluff tops so far away that Kathe was a tiny khaki figure following an ant-sized dog. Then the miniature dog became busy with her nose and tail. Several pheasants emerged from the grass, the last up being a trophy rooster. I saw the cock crumple, then two heartbeats later heard the thud of Kathe's shotgun. Minutes later, Kathe was looking my way when a rooster flared up from a draw and peeled back over my left shoulder. She saw him jolt and fall. After two heartbeats the sound of my shot reached her ears. These were prairie roosters of the second kind.

I hunted alone the following afternoon, sampling another wildlife area near where the White River empties into the Missouri. Brandy and I swept through promising cover without result before spotting a colossal cattail slough. There Brandy found scent. I was sixty yards behind her when seven pheasants stormed up, set their wings, and dropped back into the safety of the marsh's center. Brandy was still birdy. A group of about twenty birds next rose just out of gun range, topped the cattails, and settled in again. After that I was almost continuously in sight of pheasants. The marsh seemed to be composed of equal parts cattails and pheasants.

Anyone knowing me could have predicted the course of events. I was among more pheasants than I'd seen in a lifetime, yet all were flushing just out of gun range. So I went faster. Soon I was running headlong, crashing into stumps, once executing an inglorious swan dive into the muck. Because the wind was at my back, each cattail I hit released a cloud of fluff that drifted around my face like a swarm of gnats that kept pace as I dashed downwind. Fluff accumulated on my face, filled my ears, went up my nose, and got stuck in my teeth.

At long last I hauled my body out of the swamp, wheezing and snorting uncontrollably. I looked like something from a teen slasher movie: my face was a solid mask of cattail fluff with two ragged eyeholes through which I couldn't even see Brandy. My ludicrous sprint hadn't produced one shot.

I told myself that there had to be a more intelligent strategy. I turned my back on the swamp and resolved to hunt somewhere else—*anywhere* else. With so many birds around, I thought there had to be a few strays outside the marsh. That theory looked shaky when Brandy put up nineteen straight hens. Then a rooster chanced to pass overhead on his way from the cornfields to the marsh. He was a little late-hatch cock who had left his tail in some predator's jaws, but I wasn't feeling picky.

Toward dusk, our chances looked poorer. Then Brandy found scent in a grassy ditch on the perimeter of the area. In any flock, the roosters are usually the first or the last to flush. This time, four hens left the grass in front of Brandy's nose. Then up came the rooster.

With three minutes left of shooting time, we were yards from the car when a pheasant went up straight into the sun. I strained to spot a sex marker. Then he cackled, forty yards out. I fired twice with no effect. I was still watching when the bird, a dot on the horizon, soared skyward before dying mid-air and plummeting like a stone into some plowed ground. I fixed my eyes on the spot and began marching, not daring to look anywhere else. I crossed a field of cut corn, a strip of standing corn, and then a field of foxtail before reaching the plowing. There I found my rooster lying, as all such birds do, with his tail aimed like an arrow at the sky.

Kathe and I ended that first trip on a wildlife management area whose rolling contours were cleft by ragged ravines. Toward sunset I noticed a patch of grass only three inches high, cover too scruffy and inconsequential to hold a bird. I decided to hunt it out of pure whimsy. Nothing happened until we reached the tip of the grass, when all hell broke loose. A dog-sized jackrabbit galloped south with Brandy in hot but foolish pursuit. A sharptail zoomed west over my left shoulder. A rooster rose and banked north toward some standing corn. I ignored the jack, missed the sharptail, and dropped the rooster. And told myself, "Hey, I'm coming back every fall!"

South Dakota has long attracted heavy non-resident hunter traffic. When bird populations are high, motels in prime country might be booked for the opener a year in advance. I once got a room in such a motel when an Arizona hunter was felled by a heart attack and my reservation request came minutes after the manager heard he wouldn't be coming that year. Many opening week non-residents are serious hunters with dogs. Motel parking lots are full of Wisconsin Blazers with Labs in Vari-Kennels and Tennessee vans pulling dog trailers filled with ribby pointers. The structure of the season encourages visitors to stay ten days, so choice regions experience ten days of crowded hunting followed by weeks of hard scratching for a handful of veteran cocks that know the pheasant hunting game better than any man.

Some hunters are shocked to encounter commercialized pheasant hunting in South Dakota. The pheasant is a cash crop here, which is a mixed blessing. Many farmers leave a little cover for the birds so they can charge daily hunting fees. When pressure eliminates the huntable roosters on some farms, they are quietly replaced with game farm cocks. If this nation held thirty South Dakotas, there might be enough quality pheasant hunting for all hunters. Alas, it holds but one.

More than once I have vowed I wouldn't go back, yet every year I pen the season dates in my Sierra Club appointment calendar and, sooner or later, turn the blunt nose of my Isuzu Trooper west for another South Dakota pilgrimage. Nowhere else have I found what I find here: birds in abundance in gorgeous country with superb reaches of cover where a pheasant dog can do what he was born to do. The land is big and a man with legs can usually find his way to a place of poignant beauty where the dramatic encounter of bird and dog can take place just as he has seen it so often in his dreams.

"We need a strategy," I told Kathe and Jerry. "I believe a smart rooster has been beating us every day in the same place in the same way. If we lay our plans right, we might get him."

It was a dubious proposition. We hadn't seen a rooster, not even a pheasant, in this spot. But each time we swept a certain area of weeds near the Missouri, our dogs got hot. The scent would move up a slanting draw and evaporate near the top. Maybe a pheasant was eluding us by scooting up the draw. Maybe he was a rooster. Maybe we could get him by deploying our troops properly.

I drew a crude map on a Rainbow Cafe placemat. The river. The draw. Some silly looking trees to indicate the shelterbelt. I looked for totems to move on the map. "Say this jelly packet is Brandy and me. The pepper shaker is Kathe and Brinka. Jer, you're the salt cellar. Okay, the jelly packet will hunt the river and get the bird moving. If he heads up the draw he runs right into pepper shaker, who is hunting parallel to jelly packet but staggered behind a few yards. If he somehow gets by them, he'll probably make for the shelterbelt at the top of the hill. Aha, here comes salt cellar—Jerry—sneaking just inside the trees, twenty yards behind Kathe. Bango!"

Maybe, maybe, maybe.

If, if, if.

The next day, we positioned the players on the board and commenced play for real.

Brandy got scent down by the river. The scent moved up the draw although, as always, Brandy couldn't seem to get a firm fix on it. I yelled, "Watch it! He's coming!" Just then a huge old rooster flushed in Kathe's face, rising in a storm of whipping wings and percussive cackling. Kathe raised her SKB and shot. And shot again.

The rooster, unhurt, fought for altitude and veered toward the safety of the shelterbelt. At the ideal moment, Jerry stepped from the trees, exactly on the cock's path. The rooster saw him but could not alter the hurtling momentum of his flight. Jerry raised his Winchester 101 and fired at twenty-five yards. And fired again.

The rooster sailed on over the grove of trees and out of sight. I knew we'd not see him again.

When we met up again, pepper shaker and salt cellar were red-faced and apologetic. "We're sorry we missed," they chorused.

"Didja see that?" I asked. "That old rooster ran right down the pipe! We had him. It couldn't have been better!"

"We planned everything right except the best shooter was at the wrong end of the trap," said Jerry.

But the jelly packet was euphoric. "Perfect, it was perfect! It went exactly the way we diagrammed it! How often does that happen in pheasant hunting? It was dead solid perfect!"

Bill and I once spent five days in a small South Dakota town with a single cafe. It was a pleasant place run by a young couple who lived upstairs. That building encompassed their lives, for the pressure of work was such that neither of them could afford to leave the cafe except on the rarest occasion. He cooked, she waited tables, both cleaned up, and their little girl passed all her hours playing in the cafe under her parents' eyes. They seemed content with their confined lives.

Living in a tiny cell makes a person alert to minutia. One morning the cook told Bill he needed a new water pump. He'd spotted a puddle where Bill's Suburban parked that morning. A similar puddle had been left years ago by another Suburban, and it needed a water pump. He was right. We left the Suburban at a garage to be fixed while we ate breakfast. When we returned, the three mechanics broke into a triumphant jig and began cheering. "Here comes Mr. Checkbook! Call the wives and tell 'em *we eat steak tonight!*" But the charges, as they inevitably are in small-town garages, were remarkably low.

The only social contact enjoyed by the cafe couple came from the customers they attracted. The coterie of cafe regulars who hung around the place took amused interest in the two

"Minnesota boys." Conversations tended to ricochet in those small walls. A comment made in a booth would be picked up by the old guy at the counter. Then the cook would chime in through the window to the kitchen, after which the couple at the corner table would add their wisdom. It was no place to discuss secrets.

Hunting along a sheer bluff near the Missouri that year, Bill saw Ellie recoil in terror. A muscular snake with a broad head, its tail rattling zzzzzzzz, cocked to strike the young Lab. Bill shot the snake reflexively, then spent several minutes anxiously examining the corpse, wondering if he'd acted responsibly.

Bill was still unnerved hours later when we took dinner at the cafe. The cafe community chewed over the incident, declared the deceased reptile to have been a bull snake (aggressive but non-toxic), and chaffed Bill for taking the event so seriously. I threatened to advise Cindy, Bill's wife, she could get his full attention any time she needed him in the middle of the night by going zzzzzzzz in his ear. That brought the house down. Old-timers slapped their thighs, wheezed asthmatically, and daubed tears from their eyes with red kerchiefs.

Every morning and evening afterward when Bill and I appeared for a meal, from table to table there arose an omnipresent sibilant zzzzzzzz!

Years ago, an Isuzu Trooper and Bronco II lurched tortuously along a two-track trail running through a great empty plain on South Dakota's Rosebud reservation. The Isuzu veered off uphill to inspect an odd iron fence at the crest of a knoll.

Four hunters silently passed through the rusty gate. The fence defined the boundaries of an Indian cemetery. Rough wooden crosses marked most gravesites, though three granite headstones held recognizable epitaphs. One was the final resting place of Amelia Iron Shell. She had been a teenager in those desperate years when Long Hair and other cavalrymen harassed the Sioux all over these lonely hills. Her stone carried an inscription in Sioux that Kathe, with her gift for languages, understood to be a quotation from the Bible.

I wondered why the cemetery had been placed just here, on a knoll no different from hundreds of similar knolls. As I slowly turned, I understood. This place was different. By a subtle margin, it commanded the highest ground and most panoramic view of all ground in that corner of Todd County. In every direction the land fell away in languorous tan swells for miles before merging with the purple oblivion of the horizon. The person who sited the cemetery had known this land intimately, affectionately.

If you could speak to us, Amelia, you would have stories to tell. You were born in the time of the buffalo, living long enough to see them extirpated. You were raised in the spiritually nourishing life of an ancient culture. You experienced the remorseless pursuit of the pony soldiers. You suffered the profound shocks of reservation confinement and domination by an alien society. You came at last to some kind of peace with your captors, embracing their god as yours, and we can only hope you found solace in him in your final hours. *Requiescat in pace*, Amelia Iron Shell. I can imagine no lovelier place from which to regard infinity.

We exited through the iron gate. Long, polished prairie grasses danced in the soughing wind.

IOWA HOMECOMING

— • 14 • —

It is hard to see the land of your youth. Like your face in the shaving mirror, it is something you've looked at too often to see. When you travel to distant places, the terrain begins to roll differently and assumes strange colors. Exotic birds bob from the branches of exotic trees. You begin to *see*. But come back, and everything becomes too normal to command notice. At the same time, something deep in your soul says with a quiet voice, "Well, we're *home*."

I spent my first twenty-one years in central Iowa. There the landscape is arranged in the geometric symmetry of a Grant Wood painting. All that symmetry is more interesting in paintings than in one's everyday surroundings. Most of Iowa is uniformly flat, and a large percentage of Iowa's surface area is planted in corn, row after row of corn marching in file to the vanishing point like the playing-card soldiers in Disney's *Alice in Wonderland*.

As a young man I damned this land as b-o-r-i-n-g. I chafed under the midwestern obsession with being "nice" and worrying endlessly about "What will people think?" Iowans, I snorted, would rather be normal than interesting. I regarded my move to urban Minnesota as an escape from a society as crushingly bland as its unimaginative geography. I spent a decade in institutions of higher learning becoming un-Iowan. In the process I acquired a bit of wit, irony, and a veneer of sophistication about art and politics. I also acquired values some heartlanders would find shocking, with a beard to prove it.

It wrenches me now to go back to that land and its people. With each return I discover again, almost with a sense of shame, how good and kind Iowa's country people are. The Good Lord never made a more earnest, hard-working, or generous soul than the Iowa farmer. It no longer flatters me to find I have succeeded in making myself an alien among them.

The town of Winterset, like many Iowa county seats, is laid out in the New England model of a city square around a courtyard park. Stopping for gas on the way to The Rooster Factory one day, I was struck by the beauty of Winterset's nineteenth-century Italianate-Classical courthouse. Its Greek cross foundation and clockface dome rise from the court lawn as gracefully as the noble maples that flank the courthouse and cast dappled shade over the park grounds. My Ford was being gassed by a stocky pump jockey, a guy about my age, who might have been me were it not for all those college courses. I observed judiciously, "That old courthouse has lovely architecture." The station attendant drawled laconically, "Awww, she's a looker, all right."

Iowa is good pheasant country, though a frustrating place for me to hunt.

If the winters have been reasonably mild and the springs fairly normal, Iowa has birds. Iowa's fecund black loam is almost as productive of pheasants as it is of corn. Though you no longer see the clouds of birds boiling out of sloughs that I remember seeing as a kid, Iowa usually has plenty of pheasants.

Yet most Iowa farms are so small, with cover so thin and light, that my dogs and I blast through them in less time than it takes to find the right person to win permission to hunt them. Iowa farmers always tell me they've got "all kinds of cover" and that it will take me all day to see it. I'm back in an hour asking plaintively, "Is that all there is? You don't have a little more?" My dogs and I are accustomed to heroic combat in hostile jungles of wet weeds. I am a Rambo pheasant hunter at heart, happiest with a Bowie knife in my teeth and a machine gun in each hand, fighting impossible odds. Iowa is . . . well, Iowa is just too tame and tidy. I cannot find cover in Iowa that I can really engage with. Iowa is not Rambo country.

There are exceptions. I once asked permission to hunt a creekbed grown up in horseweeds and multiflora. The farmer said I was welcome to try, but I was wasting my time. Six Illinois hunters with four dogs had spent an afternoon down there without being able to harass the roosters out of that thick cover. Brandy flushed four roosters in twenty minutes, three flying where I couldn't miss them. That was in 1973, and I can still draw a good diagram of that cover. Such spots linger in memory precisely because they are so rare.

Then there is the problem presented by the typically friendly Iowa farmer who just can't say no. I cherish the fact visiting hunters can win permission to hunt most Iowa farms with a smile and a handshake. Yet that, paradoxically, is exactly where the shoe pinches. Farms that welcome all comers will soon have all their roosters shot down or run off. From mid-season on you must try to find weedy farms (which isn't easy) that have somehow been protected from hunting pressure (which is much harder) but whose owners will nevertheless let you hunt (much harder again). Groucho Marx didn't want to join the kind of club that would accept a person like him; the late season Iowa hunter wants to hunt farms that turn down people like him.

I've been too much away, spending too much time else-where. The farmers I used to know have given up on farming, died, or retired to senior citizen developments in Orlando. When I go back and stand on the porches of farms whose land I know foot by foot, I confront strangers behind screen doors.

I used to know some Iowa farm folks, knew them well. It felt right to call upon them on a November afternoon.

I think of Uncle Charley and Aunt Ruth, whom Mike Van Scoy and I met by accident one day hunting north of my college dormitory in Grinnell. Uncle Charley turned out to be an extremely distant relative of mine, though that wasn't why he welcomed us. He and Aunt Ruth behaved as if our presence were a compliment to them. By noon, Mike had three roosters and I had one (plus the anguishing memory of five misses on a cock that fanned my face on the flush). That was back in the peak of my autoloader days when I was laying out a deadly hail of shot in hopes a rooster would fly into it, trusting firepower to do what skill could not.

Mike and I stopped by the house to ask shyly for a glass of water. Instead we were treated to wedges of apple pie slathered in cinnamon ice cream and tall glasses of lemonade pressed from lemons while we watched. We left Aunt Ruth's fragrant kitchen and walked a narrow strip of unmowed corn behind the house. Three pheasants clattered into the air, much closer to limited-out Mike than to me, which caused him to hop in comic frustration. I scored my first undisputed double with a very lucky long shot on the second bird. Aunt Ruth cheered me from her porch.

Then there was the Cookie Lady. We never knew her real

name. She was the Cookie Lady because every request to hunt her farm was countered with an offer of cookies. Eating her cookies and softening the edges of her loneliness was the price Bill and I paid to walk her fields. Her place always held two or three coveys of quail in the big draws on the south side, with maybe a rooster or two in the grass and multiflora brambles up by the draw tops, and always some roosters in the weedy terraces on the west side.

The Cookie Lady, a widow, had never set foot outside a circle of forty-seven miles from the farmhouse where she was born. She married, raised a family, and worked a lifetime within that circle, never once feeling the urge to chase rainbows in the wider world.

On the Cookie Lady's farm I once shot a midget quail at close range. My shot turned the quail into a quailburger so juicy and tender that Brandy lost her composure during the retrieve. Jim Layton watched Brandy fetch the bird, calling out to me: "Don't worry Steve, Brandy's got it now. Good girl. Uh oh! Oh no, Brandy! Brandy, *NO!* Ohhh, Brandy, *evil* dog!" Jim then said, "I hate to say it, Steve, but Brandy just ate your quail. As she went by me I could see its little legs sticking out of her mouth, only they kept getting shorter and shorter." To atone for her crime, Brandy then hunted up one of the biggest cocks she and I ever killed together.

Come home, Brandy. All is forgiven. Just come home. Part of me will never understand or accept the fact you can't come home again. If you come back from wherever it is you are, I'll serve you quail twice a day.

I returned to Iowa several years ago with Minnesota conservationist, Hugh Price. It was our first hunt together. First hunts are apt to be a little snaggy. You have to sort out little habits and ground rules that old partners have settled so long ago they never think about them. Hugh and I came to sample a new business. For a fee, hunters enjoy bed-and-breakfast hospitality with a host farm family, hunting leased land nearby.

Because I stayed in college too long, I see both sides of every subject or issue. So, of course, I had mixed reactions to B & B pheasant hunting. When hunting from motels, I have a space that is almost mine. It feels right to come in from the fields, light a cigar, and roll on the floor pulling burrs from the dogs. You never feel so free when you're a farmhouse guest. The bathroom has a tub, not a shower, and the toilet will be down a flight of stairs that creak in the night as you tiptoe from the upstairs bedroom. When you get there the only reading material will be a religious magazine delineating the torments of Debbie Boone (she's not had a hit since "You Light Up My Life"; but don't worry, this has only reinforced her Faith). Yet the food is wonderful—scrumptious and too much of it—and it is charming to visit in the lives of good-hearted strangers. The farm families Hugh and I stayed with were easily the kindest people I have met in years.

We had good hunting. Not easy, but good.

I particularly remember ending the first day in some foxtail, and there are few sights more captivating than a shimmering field of foxtail in the last light of day with the sun a butterscotch globe just above the treeline. Tessie was my dog on that hunt. Over and over, Tess started a trail, lost scent, then started it again. A tricky bird was cutting a crazy path in the foxtail. We went until the foxtail stopped against a pasture with grass nibbled down by cattle. There the rooster went up, going left to right, startlingly beautiful in a sky the color of ginger ale. I almost forgot to shoot.

The next day was bone-crack cold. Snow squeaked like Polystyrene under our boots. Hugh and I walked land frozen hard as steel on two farms with pathetically little cover. I watched Hugh get one bird in a small draw. Then the dogs started up a big rooster we could see sprinting far ahead of us. Tess lost the scent but not Clipper, whose perfect field manners result from daily training sessions with his master. We followed that rooster across five fields while Hugh repeatedly whistled Clip to a halt to let us catch up. Though the cock juked and dodged and tried every trick known to roosters, Clip stuck to his trail like one of those super glues.

At last the rooster gave up on cleverness and made a dash across a grove of maples. By sheer chance I was on the far side of that grove, exactly in his path. There suddenly appeared at my feet a cock as grand and gaudy as a carousel horse. Once again I almost succumbed to the temptation to admire rather than shoot. Though he was the only bird I bagged in a long day in bitter air, I felt blessed. He was a wonderful rooster who fell victim to a perfect dog and an exceedingly lucky hunter.

The next day was even colder. Hugh and I took a typical groaning board farm breakfast by a window in a dining nook. Outside under leaden skies a wind fresh out of Manitoba sent dry snow spinning in whorls. The toasty farm home was sumptuously turned out for Christmas, a week away. To combat her empty-nest blues, our hostess had channeled her energies into crafts. Every household appliance and nearly every square inch of wall was covered with plaster plaques, afghans, pillows, homemade Christmas decorations, stuffed animals, cross-stitchery, doilies, macrame, knitted covers, needlepoint, sun catchers, figurines (human and animal, all cute), knick knacks, decorative magnets (including Polyfoam butterflies with sequined wings), and signs warning one and all against "starting anything" in this lady's kitchen.

After breakfast, Hugh and I continued to drink coffee and chew peanut brittle. I was suffering the curse of the middle-aged hunter—the readiness to trade certain animal comforts for the uncertain gains of a hunt in raw weather. After yesterday, I didn't believe in the cover. *Another cuppa coffee? Hey, don't mind if I do!* I prayed that Hugh would offer to cut the trip short. But male pride can send men to certain death in combat and this morning it kept me from bailing out of our hunt.

These things can only be delayed so long. After twelve or fourteen cups my caffeine-fevered brain raced along so briskly I was answering questions Hugh wouldn't ask until sometime in the New Year. Our host offered to escort us to the field we'd hunt. He was apologetic. An earlier party had complained about "too much cover." They couldn't roust roosters out of the weeds even with two dogs.

My ears perked up.

When I saw that farm I fell in love. A weedy creek wound a deviously twisting course through the middle. It was fed by numerous draws whose bottoms snarled and snapped with snaggy weeds. Sprinkled about were patches of set-aside, brushy field corners, grassy terraces, osage orange fencelines, and several woodlots. Such a farm could only have been planned by a very bad farmer or a very good pheasant manager. Even with Brandy I would have needed most of a day to kick out all those weeds thoroughly. It was . . . Bless me, it was Rambo country!

Just then the sun broke out of the clouds. I was suddenly twenty-three again, with the elastic legs of a kangaroo and a high bounding heart. Tess and I charged off on our own, leaving Hugh and Clipper to work at a more reasonable pace.

Our first rooster flushed behind my back and quite far away in some standing corn. He offered only a glimpse of his body when I whipped around to snap off a shot. I was thrilled to find him lying on his back between the corn rows, feet up, looking as peaceful as if he'd been laid out for a viewing. Then it was Tess's turn to shine, trailing a cock that led us a complicated chase along the creek and up a draw to its bitter end. I almost made the classic beginner's booboo of failing to work out the very last few inches of cover.

Hugh and I crossed paths about noon. Hugh, too, had two birds. He wanted to knock off to have lunch—a reasonable request—but I had to disappoint him. I had hit my stride, endorphins coursed in my veins, and there was the whole shaggy north half of the farm we hadn't touched yet. Wild horses couldn't have dragged me from that field.

Tess and I took off again. We walked up and down, flushing seven hens, before Tess picked up a thread of scent that led by a serpentine course to a nasty ditch full of weeds the height of young trees. I thought, "This is rooster cover." It was.

Driving home, every muscle between my eyes and my toes throbbed with glorious pain. Hugh mused aloud that he was going to have to bring his old hunting partners out of moth balls because I, frankly, hadn't worked out that well. I was too much of a damned young tiger to hunt sensibly. He said, half seriously, he'd missed a rooster at six paces because I had kept him so long from his lunch that he was wobbly with hunger.

Outside the car windows, in the fading pearly light of evening, the Iowa landscape whirred past. Flat, flat, flat. Corn, corn, corn. Scattered here and there in that infinity of corn were little farmsteads flanked by sheltering groves where, I knew, pheasants were at this very moment trailing in from the snowy fields to sleep where winter couldn't touch them.

It looked bland. Tame. Symmetrical. Normal. And I heard the little voice that said, "Well, we're *home!*"

A COLD, LONELY DEATH

———— • 15 • ————

We loved hunting not wisely but too well, Brandy and I. Perhaps it was inevitable that some day we would pay the price for our intemperate zeal.

On the year Brandy and I fought the marsh, Kathe, Jerry, and I met to hunt the Missouri Breaks country. A December blizzard and frigid spring had blighted bird numbers, producing a rare year of difficult hunting in that bird-rich land.

Yet there is no bad hunting when you are with good friends. And any hunting you get from a twelve-year-old dog is to be cherished. Brandy capered through the cover with the joy and drive of a youngster. After all our years together, we had attained a oneness that let us coordinate movements as unconsciously as the fingers of the same hand. In a day of hunting, I

133

would only use my voice to praise her. We claimed a few roosters, each of them appreciated all the more because they came hard and because most were magnificent old cocks with tails like windsocks.

I only regretted that our scouting report would be so discouraging for the three Minnesota hunters driving several hundred miles to join me for the second half of my hunt. Kathe and Jerry returned home to be replaced by Bill and two friends, John and Jamie. We mulled over strategies when they arrived. In order to find a region with huntable rooster numbers, we split the party the next day. John and Jamie drove north while Bill and I explored fields south and west of town.

There Bill and I, stopping for gas, spent nearly an hour in a prairie ghost town. Its six sun-bleached buildings resembled the set of *The Last Picture Show.* The town's sole inhabitant was an old woman, herself as weathered and gray as what was left of her town. She ran a gas station and general store. In a reedy voice she described the slow death of a town that once throbbed with vitality. As we left, I bought a Baby Ruth. Its caramel core was brittle and its chocolate skin chalky gray.

Though Bill and I hunted hard, with less than three hours of light left we hadn't seen a rooster. We closed the day on one of South Dakota's huge public hunting areas. Many years earlier, Brandy and I had enjoyed a daffy hunt near here, the hunt that masked me in cattail fluff.

This wildlife area has a great expanse of undulating prairie that drops to meet the White River near its juncture with the Missouri. Below the grassland lies a vast bulrush and cattail marsh. Looking across that marsh, Bill and I saw a large island of dry ground overgrown with willows. We formed our plan hastily. Perhaps the willows had become a sanctuary for pheasants. By crossing the marsh we might reach ground no other bird hunter had tramped. It was a desperate plan, born of desperation. Bill said, "A Minnesotan doesn't think he's pheasant hunting until he gets wet, so we're fated to give it a try."

The first marsh crossing was quick and painless. Bill and I walked less than a hundred yards in weedy water that rarely topped our boots. Because the prevailing westerly winds had tipped the rushes over in the direction we were walking, west to east, we slipped through them easily. I noted it wouldn't be so fun when we came out and had to buck against the grain of the weeds.

Our plan fell apart as soon as we hit the island. Dead willows lay about in a jackstraw jumble as though someone had spilled a box of giant kitchen matches. The willows were so brittle I could shatter them with my knees, but our thunderous progress would never put us near a rooster. Worse, I saw the timber was not cover that would tempt a pheasant to hold for a close flush.

Bill and I almost immediately encountered a deer hunter up a tree. He was disgusted to have two nutty bird hunters ruining his evening. Bill veered to his right, I veered left. Moments later, we blundered into a second deer hunter. Murmuring apologies, I drifted deeper into the willows, farther from Bill, who again moved to his right.

I didn't see Bill after that. That happens in heavy cover. With legal shooting time growing short, Brandy and I tore through the trees, looking for birdy weeds. I crashed through dead willows that Brandy floated over with elfish ease. She twice bounced up pheasants just out of range.

An hour later it was clear that we would never find what we sought. I hated to give up without taking a shot, but it seemed the birds had won all rounds this day. We angled back toward the marsh to make the crossing that would reunite us with Bill and the car.

Brandy and I found the marsh again a mile or two from our original crossing. The pale November sun hung just above the bluffs over the western edge of the marsh. We'd need to hustle to reach the west side with any light left. The marsh looked wider here, but standing on the low ground I couldn't tell how far the wet part extended. We faced a continuous sea of fea-

tureless marsh grass, most of it over my head. I considered returning to where we'd crossed first, but that would send us
bumbling through the deer stands again.

I fluffed the hair on Brandy's head. "Looks like we're going
to get wet, old girl." And we entered the marsh.

As expected, we had to force a path through the weeds because they were intertwined and folded over pointing toward
us. I clawed at them to unbraid the strands. Brandy left me
once to pursue a cock that flushed outside shotgun range.

The water got deeper until it filled my field boots. Soon the
water also carried a thin crust of ice. I smiled ruefully as I re-
called articles I'd written about the joys of chasing roosters in
marshes. I told Brandy, "Some folks would enjoy seeing the
old swamp lover in this mess."

We thrashed on, deeper and deeper into the marsh's dark
center. At first I simply slashed through the shell ice with my
shins. Then that became too painful. The ice became so thick
I had to stomp a path in it. Brandy had given up hunting and
was shivering in the channel I'd kicked. The ice was too weak
to bear her weight and too crusty for her to make her own way.

The ice got thicker. I was reduced to punching a path with
my shotgun stock. Its finish began to flake, but I never cared
for that plastic finish anyway. The sun drooped lower. From
my position down in the weeds I could see no more than fifteen
yards ahead. The rushes at the edge of my vision seemed
lighter, leading me to hope we had finally walked through the
wet area and could dash to the car in comfort. But always, as I
moved ahead, the lighter weeds remained the same distance
ahead, taunting me. On and on we labored, not knowing if dry
land was a dozen feet ahead or much farther away.

Brandy and I had toiled in icy weeds a long time before it
occurred to me we were in trouble. Having come so far, I
couldn't face the prospect of fighting our way all the way back
out so we could hike to the site of the original crossing and do
it all over. I couldn't let go of the hope that we would reach dry

ground soon if we kept plunging forward. Plunging forward was all we had known to do for a dozen years.

At some point I knew that Brandy and I had passed through a door into a world we'd never known before. On the other side of the door we had worried about such things as staying comfortable, finding pheasants, and meeting friends on time. Where we were now, the real issue was whether Brandy or I would live to see the morning sun. There is a limit to how long a man or dog can function while losing warmth to cold water. A countdown had begun against us when we stepped into the ice water.

Fear and frustration mounted in me until I felt I could climb my rage like a ladder and learn at long last how far we had to go to reach dry ground. The watery part of the marsh obviously stopped at the base of the bluffs in the distance, though I hoped with increasing desperation that safety lay much closer than that. But what if it didn't? What if water extended all the way to the bluffs? What if the water got an inch or two deeper before it shallowed?

Then Brandy lost her legs. Courage and loyalty were no match, ultimately, for all that ice water. Her legs locked so tight she could neither walk nor swim. A grim pattern had been set. I would bash a narrow path through ice and weeds, then return to drag Brandy's rigid body until I had to leave her to hack ice again. By holding her chin high she could keep her nose above water, just barely.

I began to fire distress signals, a series of three spaced shots. *Blam, Blam, Blam!* Nobody could hear them, but I was in the worst trouble of my life and wanted to say so in the loudest way possible. My shots evoked the only noise Brandy made that evening. She moaned in frustration at her inability to retrieve what I was shooting.

As I thrashed and chopped I noted I was close to drowning in knee-deep water. As long as I stood I was perfectly safe, but within minutes my legs would cramp up like Brandy's. Then it would soon be over. Twice I threw Brandy up over my shoulders but found it impossible to bash a path with her there. The attempt was foolish, as the water draining off her and over my chest was deadly cold.

Soon I struggled with decisions as terrible in their own way as the marsh. I wondered if I should abandon Brandy or carry her and leave my gun behind. What should I try to save, the cloudy-eyed old springer or the shotgun? That nasty debate was brief. I simply couldn't break ice without the shotgun. A more serious issue was whether I—a husband and father—had the right to risk my life with efforts to save Brandy's.

More distress signals. *Blam, blam, blam!* We struggled on. *Blam, blam, blam!* I began looking at Brandy with grief in my face. Shuddering uncontrollably, her eyes glowing with intensity, she was literally an inch from drowning. Finally I was down to four shells, enough for a last distress signal with one left for Brandy. I kept asking, *"How bad does it have to get before I shoot her?"*

Blam, blam, blam!

Then I heard a voice. From somewhere in the dark, a man's voice said, "Are you in trouble?"

I yelled, "Yes! I'm out here with an old dog. I don't know if either of us will make it. Please stay there."

The voice: "Do you have waders?"

"No. How far does the wet marsh go?"

"I'm standing at the edge. Just keep coming."

Awww no! Damn, damn, damn! I saw him now, a dim object in the failing light. The worst possible case was the one we faced. Water and ice extended all the way to the base of the western bluffs. So far. So very far.

We hacked forward several minutes longer when my worst fears were realized. The water became deeper. I chattered cheerfully to Brandy, though twice I fingered my trigger and debated using "Brandy's" shell. She obviously wasn't going to make it. The water was too deep, the distance too far, the progress too slow.

Then I saw a muskrat house—the only rat house in that whole marsh—lying directly in our path. I broke ice to it, returned for Brandy, and boosted her to safety. I was shocked to find how much trouble I had climbing up to join her. My hands shredded the top of the rat house before seizing on something solid enough that I could haul myself up. I seemed to have been Novocained from the hips down. I pummeled my legs with frenzied fists, feeling nothing.

Night fell. Stars emerged. I hopped wildly to regain the use of my legs. When I slid off the rat house back into black water I knew Brandy would have to remain behind. I would come back for her or perhaps offer money to the stranger to rescue her. I couldn't meet Brandy's eyes when I said, "So long, old friend. See you in a while. *Stay! Stay!*"

I made better time without Brandy. Now the water was almost waist-deep. I rushed. Halfway to safety my legs began cramping painfully. I saw I might drown sixty yards from shore, and my anonymous friend could not reach me in time. I forced myself to move slowly to keep my legs sound.

It was pitch black when I stumbled out of the water and began running in circles to force blood back in my legs, babbling about the dog I'd left behind. There was no possibility of returning for Brandy, and no rational man would enter that ice water without waders to rescue her. My last sensible act was to break off the top of a little tree to mark the spot where a ragged path led out through a morass of weeds and ice to a muskrat house.

The trek to the car was nightmarish. The hunter lent me his coat and—for what reason, I don't recall—a bandanna. Maybe I was crying. He confided he hadn't thought I would make it to shore. He assured me Brandy would walk out when the night air made the ice thick enough for safe travel. I was just as sure she would come off the house and die thrashing in shards of ice. Back at the car, an ashen-faced Bill awaited me.

Then came the tears. Tears of fear. Tears of relief. Tears of exhaustion. Tears of gratitude. Above all, tears for Brandy. I had deserted the best buddy I'd known in life, leaving her to a cold, lonely death. Bill drove twenty miles before I could find the voice to tell our story.

At the motel I plunged into a tub and ran steaming water into it for half an hour. The better I felt physically, the worse I felt for Brandy. Bill had organized a rescue party before I had dressed. Local game wardens loaned us chest waders and lanterns. We were soon driving back to the management area.

Four of us struck off across the spooky prairie toward the marsh. I tried to make small talk to disguise my anxiety. How long would Brandy stay on the rat house? Had she already drowned? How long could an exhausted old dog, soaked in ice water, survive in November night air even if she stayed put?

We were still high on the prairie when I heard Brandy barking. Ah, that sound, that sound! How often I have hated that sound when she barked at inconvenient times! Now her barking was sweeter to my ears than the music of angels. She was alive! So far, she was alive. We conferred. Brandy's barking probably meant she had heard us. She might be tempted by our voices to make a doomed break for shore. We quit speaking. The black marsh fell silent again.

Finding the path in the ice wasn't easy. I'd been incoherent on the way out, and now the world looked bizarre in our whirling lantern beams. The bluffs that had mocked my progress that evening, though their image was fixed in my mind, were invisible in the night sky. We hiked the edge of the marsh in strained silence.

Then something looked odd. My light caught a small tree, its top snapped and inverted. Below it, a ragged channel pointed toward the dark heart of the marsh. Brandy hadn't barked for half an hour, a fact we all noted but avoided mentioning. Bill and Jamie donned waders and slipped into the water. I told Bill, "If Brandy is dead, please leave her there. I don't know a better place to bury her." Brandy and I had known great happiness not far from here one bright November afternoon.

For several minutes we could hear no sound from the marsh except the swish of boots in water and the grinding of tectonic plates of ice. My fingers played over some cellophaned meat patties in my pockets. I prayed I'd have cause to open them. Out in the darkness, Bill's voice said, "*Stay*, Brandy. *Stay*." Did he see her? Or was he just taking precautions? Then my heart raced as Bill called lovingly, "Goood girl!"

Bill found Brandy perched regally on the rat house in her "library lion" position, her head high, paws thrust forward. She had licked herself dry and had no problems worse than a full bladder and an empty stomach. Bill carried her to shore cradled in his arms like a child.

Four lantern lights bobbed giddily through the darkness of a prairie under a starshot sky. A startled family of white-tailed deer turned to mark our passing. Judging us harmless, they dropped their heads to resume grazing. Dimly visible now and then on the fringes of our beams, a small white shape could be seen gamboling through the tall grass. An old springer was hunting again.

PRAIRIE RATTLER

Jim Marti lives on some prairie north of Bismarck, North Dakota. A large, modern kennel facility stands nearby, and if you visit Burnt Creek Kennels you might decide Jim has given his dogs nicer quarters than he's given himself. Jim is a hunter, trainer, prairie poet, columnist for *Pheasants Forever*, and conservationist. Above all, Jim is a breeder of hunting English setters, dogs that are stylish, birdy, and well-intentioned.

You notice two things when you hunt with Jim. His gun, an SKB side-by-side 20, has a flame orange forend and buttstock. Jim trains as he hunts. Since he often must drop his gun in the weeds and run to correct a dog, he's learned the wisdom of carrying a bright gun. You notice, too, that Jim carries that gun crooked over his arm with the action open. He closes the action only when a dog strikes a point. For Jim, hunting does not exist apart from dog work, and he has no interest in shooting roosters his dogs have not found and worked successfully.

My first contact with Jim came when he phoned to point out errors in the pointing dog material of *Modern Pheasant Hunting.* He said I had "got it all wrong about pointing dogs and pheasants," adding charitably, "but we're used to that because everyone else gets it wrong, too." Then he ordered several copies of my flawed book to donate to his Pheasants Forever chapter.

The incident is a microcosm of an unusual but cherished friendship. Jim and I could hardly be less alike. I am mushy and forgiving; Jim is fiercely dedicated to high standards. I always see the merit in an antagonist's argument; Jim's hobby is castigating editors, photographers, politicians, game managers, and bureaucrats for their egregious errors. I am thin-skinned and eager to please; Jim is an old prairie rattler. Rage is as natural to him as it is unnatural to me. When I look upon this society's tragic abuse of the natural world, I grieve. Jim sees the same things and thunders like an Old Testament prophet.

All we share is a passion for pheasants and pheasant dogs. It has been enough. Meeting Jim, I experienced something I've not felt before or since. As we studied each other, I thought, "You have it, don't you? *You have the fire.* After all these years, I've found someone else who knows what it is to have the fire."

Though the fire might be banked a little these days, Jim once burned with my intemperate ardor for pheasant hunting. I've long dreamed of hunting pheasants thirty days in a row. Jim did it. With characteristic candor, he remembers, "It got to be like going to the office. I'd get up in the morning and say, 'Awww, do I (bleepin') *haffta* go again?'"

My first hunt with Jim was memorable for many things, including mixed bags (roosters, sharptails, and Hungarian partridge) and the governor. North Dakota's governor, George "Bud" Sinner, joined us one day. That was my first hunt with a political celebrity. Frankly, I had misgivings. I expected aides to trot out the governor, put someone else's bird and gun in his hands, and turn our hunt into a photo opportunity. Instead, Governor Sinner distinguished himself by walking hard and making a clean kill with a long shot on a wild-flushing rooster. He made quite a splash, too, by jumping across three feet of a four-foot creek. The governor gamely continued hunting for several hours with creek water gurgling in his boots. This poor nation needs forty-nine more governors like that.

When Jim saw me arguing with Pogo on the fourth day of our first North Dakota hunt (she wanted to spend the day in the motel watching Road Runner cartoons), he told me, "You know, you've got the wrong dog. That's a good dog for an old man who hunts a couple of hours on Sundays." "I know." A day later, Halloween Day, Spook entered my life.

A wriggling mass of puckish energy, he barely filled my open hand. I studied his face, seeking clues about the dog he would some day become. Spook gnawed my thumb pensively while cocking at eye at me. I hoped, but could not then know, that silent messages of greatness were written in the genetic code of Spook's tiny cells.

Spook returned to North Dakota a year later to show the home folks how he had turned out. There he met Wayfarer's Rex, Jim's gunning partner and Spook's own grandfather. The two setters sampled each other's scent, found it familialy agreeable, and turned at once to more important matters. On that trip, thirteen-month-old Spook successfully pointed North Dakota roosters, Huns, and sharptails. He had already pointed South Dakota prairie chickens, Wisconsin ruffed grouse, and Minnesota woodcock, and was soon to add Iowa quail and wild turkeys. (When Spook discovered turkeys, thirteen of them in an Iowa CRP field, I had trouble getting him to condescend to hunt "little" birds like roosters again.)

On one hazy, wind-tossed afternoon I'll never forget, Jim and I were privileged to hunt with a grand old dog and a wonderfully precocious youngster.

I remember how that day began. As we slid shotguns from their cases and donned hunting jackets, Jim said, "Well, let's see if the Spook pup is half the dog you say he is." I nodded my head toward a scruffy copse of volunteer elms. There Spook was standing, taut and purposeful, the feathering of his upthrust tail throbbing in the wind. A hen pheasant lay snugged in the grass before his nose. Said Jim softly, "I do believe our little boy is becoming a fine man."

We shot four roosters that afternoon, but they were incidental to the dog work, which was as pretty as I've seen or expect to see. Two white setters laced the cover with ecstasy and efficiency, working difficult birds with persistent skill, and we had to look hard to tell which dog was which. Even Jim, the fervent perfectionist, shook his head and said, "I don't know how it could have been better. I don't see how they could have done it better." And when Spook nailed a footloose old cock on a weedy hillside, Rex was proud to honor his point. Those dogs gave us a mental snapshot to be carried forever: grandson and grandfather standing together with high heads and tails as the rooster whipped free of the grass and rode the prairie wind to safety.

Two years later Spook and I hunted that same ground. Rex had grown older, stiffer, and more affectionate. But he still hunted and still hit his points with the suddenness and finality that won so many trials for him as a youngster. On one particular hunt, Spook and I went alone. We moved through a field of waving weeds so wide even Spook's distance-eating lope couldn't cover the whole thing. He disappeared over a knoll.

When I topped that knoll I saw my dog on point over a hundred yards away. I walked briskly to join him. Spook from time to time turned his head from the scent, imploring me with expressive eyes to join him. By the time I arrived he was flagging and grinning self-consciously. The bird had moved.

I released him. Spook went into a cloverleaf search pattern, venturing out to make new contact with the bird, then returning again to the original scent before striking out in a new direction. I simply watched. He needed no help from me. Then he froze again, catwalked one step forward and went so rigid that if I'd moved his tail it would have shattered like crystal. I stepped four feet in front of him. The rooster—no, two roosters!—cackled into the bright sky.

Jim was sitting in his truck at the end of the field, slipping Rex a piece of bologna sandwich, when he heard the distant shots. "Hmmm! One shot, a pause, then another shot. Whaddya think, Rexie? When our partner shows up, will he have a swagger in his step? Will he be hard to live with?"

Jim once wrote me about birds he remembered and memories he had of some of the dogs buried on the hill overlooking the creek behind his place. For this book, Jim asked me to delete some of his expletives.

"1975 was the year of the 22-Minute Pheasant: 22 minutes on the trail of one wily ringneck before we got him pinned against a hay stack right on the edge of the Knife River. When I looked back up the 40-acre alfalfa field we had hunted it looked—because of the frost—like a berserk spiderweb wherever we had walked and knocked the frost down. We had walked up and down, up and down several times following that mad dog and madder rooster. Not a kid or puppy bird, for a fact.

"I had a fast dog then, Jessie James, who left smoke trails through the grass. Later, the pup Ruff turned out to be a very fine pheasant dog, although a world different from that crazy pheasant-murdering Jessie. I don't miss Jessie that much, but I can't take a step without missing goofy Ruff, who was so damn loyal to me. One man, blessed in the same decade with two setters that were diametrically opposed in method and who produced exactly the same number of birds to the gun.

"Sometimes I think I'll go dig up Jessie and Ruff and Hemingway and Truman and possibly that wonderfully crazy Moonshine Crockett and we'll do it all over again, the same or better.

We'll go again and go and go until we all drop in a heap for the magpies to have. With one last rooster clenched in our teeth!"

Jim concluded that letter with a paean to the importance of a land that is healthy and rich enough in weeds to support pheasants and other wild things:

"How do you explain all that to the younger coming generation? I can't because they think I'm mad. I can only nudge and shove and threaten my own government to create the habitat that creates the birds that create the men and women that create the fun and drama and tears and laughter and the playing out of life and death in the tall grasses of that place way up yonder on the sidehill north of the Jones place where we used to pick the cacti out of old Sam's ass and kill those beautiful shocking roosters."

Rage on, old man, rage on.

SEEKING THE PERFECT PHEASANT GUN

———— • 17 • ————

I used to hunt pheasants with a fellow who shot a Model 24 Winchester. The Model 24 was a beer drinker's double, a functional gun with mulish lines. My friend's 24 was not especially pretty because he used the receiver to jam down the top strand of barbed wire fences he crossed. But he was used to his gun. It shot well enough to kill sixty pheasants a year, plus more than that number of quail and rabbits.

Then my friend moved to a pricey suburb, and the scarred-up old double became an embarrassment. "My neighbors got guns that cost more than my car," he told me. He ordered a middling fancy Browning Citori. While not a collector's piece, the new gun was a lovely thing he could uncase without blushing.

A year later I asked how the new gun was working out. "Terrible," he moaned, "just terrible. I'm going back to my old 24. The stock is different somehow and I can't hit anything. You know what's worse—all of a sudden I don't know how to get across a fence!"

Draw your own lesson from that tale. It reminds me that hunters are so idiosyncratic that the ideal pheasant gun for one fellow will be totally unsuitable for another. There is, in other words, no "perfect" pheasant gun for all hunters. We all have to search for the gun that suits us and our own way of hunting. Then, for many of us, the real trick is to recognize that gun and not sell it in a foolish effort to get something better.

To further illustrate this point, let me describe the gun that would be perfect for me—and shockingly inadequate and unacceptable for most hunters.

My perfect pheasant gun would be a light 12 with a straight English grip, fairly high comb, and just a smidgeon of cast-off. The wood wouldn't just have pretty figure, it would be downright erotic. Since I don't use my receiver to cross wire fences, I'd like some engraving, perhaps some tasteful scroll work with an anatomically correct setter on one side and a plausible rooster on the other. Give me a raised but not ventilated rib, a tang safety, and a forearm somewhere between a beavertail and a splinter. A crisp trigger would be nice, along with a selective ejector and a choke of about thirty-four percent.

Sounds nice, right? But did you notice my perfect pheasant gun is a *single shot*? And for good reason.

As a kid, I shot a single 20 and shot it well. It was sweet to carry and quick to mount. I have fond memories of the afternoon my little 20 cracked down three successive roosters in front of my father before he could shoulder his massive 12 pump.

Of course, I saw the 20 as a "kid's gun" and couldn't wait to get rid of it. I spent almost two years mowing lawns to buy a Browning Auto-5. And for a dozen years, my shooting went straight to Hell. I blamed the gun. In desperation I mounted a Poly-Choke. I goofed around with the stock, building a singularly homely Monte Carlo from masking tape and Naugahyde. Nothing helped. I finally blamed the square receiver and began plotting another gun purchase.

Then I thought the matter over. Perhaps I was spraying lead all over the sky because, subconsciously, I was pretty impressed by the fact that I could miss once and still have four more at-bats. So I stuck a "duck plug" in my gun, though it hurt to throw away half the firepower I'd earned cutting all those lawns. The duck plug accomplished what the Poly-Choke and stock tinkering could not. I stopped shooting like a Chicagoland gangster and began looking at my roosters. And they began to drop.

Years later, in a rare fit of candor, I tried to remember all the roosters I'd bagged with my third shell. The total was one. Either I scored with the first or second shot or I missed with all three. I used that analysis as an excuse to buy my first double. And I began instantly to shoot better with two shells than I had with three.

I now have carried a 12 gauge SKB over/under for fifteen years. I suspect it will be my last pheasant gun because it shoots so well for me that I can't make a case for buying something else. The stock fits my physique, and the chokes (improved and modified) suit my hunting style. I harbor no delusions about its beauty. The rococo silver receiver looks exactly like a cap gun I once owned. But the SKB is an honest, reliable gun that now carries fifteen years of fond memories. If I'd cut a notch for each rooster it claimed, there wouldn't be much stock left.

I could only improve on the SKB by finding that mythical high grade single shot. A single shot is all I need because I shoot over a pointer. While I rarely miss with the second barrel, I still tend to dump the first barrel. Having only one shot would concentrate my mind on that critical first shot and raise the level of my shooting overall.

Of course, most hunters regard two or three quick shots as the minimum standard for a pheasant gun. There was even a time when bird numbers and hunting styles made a fourth or fifth shell useful. The big cornfield drives of my childhood sometimes gave a hunter five or six shots in one ferocious salvo. I recall seeing four roosters up and in range simultaneously. Modern pheasant hunting involves more walking, less shooting, and fewer views of more than one rooster in the air.

A single shot would deny me the chance—rare though it is— of shooting a double. I could live with that. A recent pheasant double still haunts me. Brandy and I approached a finger of cattails projecting into prairie grass. The marsh began to roar with pheasant wings. I dropped a pair of cocks, reloaded, and shot a late-riser.

I knew it wouldn't be easy to find those birds, though all fell with limp necks. I have trouble enough marking two falls simultaneously, let alone three. For some reason the cattails had all let down their fluff that year, carpeting the marsh floor in a foot-high layer of cottony fuzz. We turned three good retrievers loose in the area. Every attempt to inhale bird scent caused the dogs to go into sneezing fits. I eventually pocketed one rooster and left, I'm sure, two stone-dead birds for the foxes. I'll never try for a double again unless the ground beneath them is uncommonly clean and open—which means I'll probably never try for another double.

When I wrote my first pheasant book I was younger and much wiser than I now know myself to be. In my gun advice I excluded only two types of shotguns—single shots and bolt actions—as inadequate for pheasants. Having eaten half that advice, I'll now eat the other half. The best pheasant field shot I've watched in action used a Mossberg bolt 12-gauge, a gun I once considered unacceptably slow on repeat shots and about as pleasant to swing as an ironing board.

Theoretically, bolts are slow, but my friend could cycle his almost as fast as any pump. Under circumstances too complicated to explain here, he once poured three shots at close range into the side of a speeding Porsche, and Porsches are *quick*. My friend could snick his bolt quickly enough to crack off three shots on one rooster rise, though he never needed to.

How could he shoot so well with such a gun? I offer two suggestions. First, he was so familiar with his Mossberg that it pointed for him as naturally as his eyes. Not that he shot every gun that well. When his old bolt burst a barrel, my friend bought a new Remington 1100 that he absolutely couldn't shoot. Then he spotted a rusty old used Mossberg bolt in a gun shop. He was delighted to trade the gleaming new 1100 for it, even-Steven.

My friend once was trapped behind North Korean infantry lines, forced to eat grass for nine days—an experience that left him forever obsessed with food. When a cock went up in all its cackle-flapping glory, he didn't see a wildly exciting game bird but a deeply coveted meal. He hunted more like an owl than a human, with perfect concentration and no complicating emotions.

The point is not that we all should shoot bolt actions. We all just need to find what we shoot well and stick with it. Ultimately, for most shooters, shooting well does not have a great deal to do with fine details of our choice of weapon. Shooting well on pheasants or other flying game mainly has to do with shooting well, which comes from practice.

Let's examine the various parameters of an upland shotgun. We'll look for those qualities that define the perfect gun for pheasant hunters. We won't find them.

As indicated, any action type you like and handle well is right for you. I believe most hunters would shoot well with some sort of two-barreled gun. Most, not all. So just suit yourself.

What about gun weight? I am not proud that I once wrote that a pheasant gun should weigh seven pounds. Writers like myself who might not lift anything heavier in an average week than a beer are apt to praise light guns. Yet I've hunted with a fellow who fills a size 15 EEE boot. John can stuff a huge autoloader with magnums and swing it as deftly as any imported 28 with girlish proportions. In his arms, a seven pound gun would feel as twitchy as guns weighing less than six pounds feel in mine. Choose the weight you feel comfortable carrying, somewhere between six and eight pounds.

What about gauge? The pheasant is a remarkably hardy bird. Stories I could offer as evidence are too gruesome for public view, but we all know a rooster is mighty hard to separate from his soul. The "use enough gun" maxim points to the 12 as the ideal pheasant gauge. But the 20 gauge is only slightly less potent, while the 16 is so close it is pointless to bicker about differences.

I remember a particular rooster. Jim Marti's canny old setter, Rex, hit and broke about four quick points in a row along a North Dakota creekbed. Jim yelled that a bird was running and we should head him off. Bill and I dashed ahead of Rex, but the rooster was ahead of us and out quite a bit when it broke. Our first two shots rolled the bird. Then at about fifty yards, the third shot smacked him down. If the weak hits hadn't been from my 12 gauge and the crushing final hit from Bill's 20, we might have jumped to a false conclusion about the efficacy of the two gauges. On paper, the 20 and 16 should be "almost" as good as the 12. In the field, I see no difference.

I once considered the 28 to be a sub-marginal pheasant gauge. And, alas, I said so in print. Now two friends enjoy telling me how wrong I was. They've never shot better than they do with their new 28s.

Is there such a thing as the "right" or "best" choke for pheasants?

I used to champion open chokes with the fervor of the recently converted. Most pheasants I've seen hit or missed were between twenty and thirty yards from the shooter. That convinced me the improved cylinder was the perfect pheasant choke. And I became obnoxious on the subject.

I keep my mouth shut these days. To pick the right choke you must predict the range of your next shot. Of course, roosters are masters at making such predictions look foolish; it's what being a pheasant is all about. The whole issue of choke choice is complicated by a number of important variables rarely mentioned in technical discussions of ideal chokes for pheasant hunters.

One major variable is hunting style. If you hunt with gangs in drives, your average shot might be long enough to require a full choke. If you hunt heavy cover with a flusher, a modified might suit you. The man who only takes roosters holding for points will be deadly with an improved cylinder.

It matters where you hunt, too. My faith in open chokes arises from my penchant for hunting marshes. I don't feel I've begun a hunt until I'm out somewhere where duck boats go. Roosters in monster swamps, like tigers in tall grass, offer close shots. Friends who hunt Kansas stubble fields say there are days they couldn't make a clean kill without screwing in the full choke tube.

Arguments about ideal choke usually ignore shooter psychology. Two friends grew up shooting ruffed grouse and never learned to slow down for roosters. One of those quick-draw artists could be on his third shot when a cock was little more than head-high. Two other friends are as deliberate on the shot as poker players in a high stakes game. They shoot full chokes well enough to go whole seasons without a miss or cripple.

There's another factor that never gets discussed in theoretical debates about choke (or gauge, for that matter). My friend who shot the bolt so well was a veteran hunter who knew pheasants. At critical moments he was always positioned to take good shots because experience taught him how roosters think. If you are getting only forty-five yard shots, you might need a 12 with a full choke to get clean kills. More likely what you really need is more bird savvy, or perhaps a phlegmatic short-hair with restricted range. Done right, pheasant hunting is not a long-distance game.

Like gauge and gun weight and action type, choke cannot be chosen by consulting the Platonic ideal of Pheasant Gun. Choose a choke after assessing what would be appropriate for you, given where and how and when you hunt. Then watch the results. If you either miss or pulverize most birds, your choke is too tight. If you lose a lot of cripples, your choke might be too open (although many cripples are birds fringe-hit with overly tight chokes).

What about stock fit? Most pheasants present a rising target, and far more roosters are missed low than high. That argues for a gun stocked high to shoot high. But while early-season birds often flush from low and go up, late-season roosters often flush off high ground and fly down. It is easy to shoot over those guys with any gun, let alone one rigged to shoot high. And I'm uneasy with the notion we should jigger stock fit to compensate for lazy swinging. Your gun should shoot where you look.

Most people I've known who made a big deal of stock fit were marginal shooters seeking a quick fix. They were over-weight, under-dogged, or simply inept at shooting flying. That observation long ago made me a cynic about hunters who be-lieve there is a gun with a magic set of specifications that could transform them into the sensational shooters they've always been in their fantasies.

I recently had lunch with a friend who challenged that cyn-icism. He'd solved his shooting woes by switching to a comely 28 over/under. "This little gun really does it, Steve. I just don't miss now. Grouse, quail, roosters—it does a job on all of them." He added darkly, "And you *know* how I used to shoot."

"Well, ummm, I've seen you hit some and miss some."

"*SHITTY!* I was *shitty!* But not now, believe me!"

So it happens. Most hunters eventually find that a certain gun or set of stock specifications allow us to shoot as well as our abilities permit. Some of us discover those specifications by getting measured by an expert. Most of us get there by dinking around with guns until one day we pick one up and absolutely powder a clay target with it. Then we grin and say to the stock, "Well, *hello!* You took your sweet time coming into my life!"

The American sportsman has always sought to buy competence, not earn it, which means pheasant hunters are overly fascinated with shotguns and insufficiently committed to practice. Many shotguns are sold because a hunter thinks he can solve shooting problems by getting a gun with a little more of this or a little less of that. There are worse vices. And some that are even more expensive.

So far, we have narrowed our search for the ideal pheasant gun down to every gauge between 28 and 12 in every possible action type. We've concluded the gun's weight should fall somewhere between six and eight pounds. The ideal choke, we learned, is improved cylinder or full. Or anything in between. And we finally decided the perfect stock might be straight or crooked, or whatever fits a particular shooter. That nails it down pretty tightly, I think. In all other matters, you are free to follow your heart.

In this discussion there is little to give comfort to the fellow telling his wife he "needs" a four thousand dollar shotgun for pheasants. But if there is no reason to spend so much, there is no reason (beyond the obvious) not to. Some folks believe an excellent bird should only be hunted with an excellent gun. It is a pretty sentiment, for those who can afford it.

We all have to pursue in our own way the perfect gun for our pheasant hunting. It is an odyssey that has few signposts to mark the way. Instead, it is a highly personal quest, much like the search for the perfect spouse. Some of us get lucky the first time around. Some of us are doomed to try many times until we at last find the right one.

Many of us go on searching for that elusive ideal until one day we realize perfection is a mighty suspicious goal. And, hell, the one we're with is probably better than we deserve anyway.

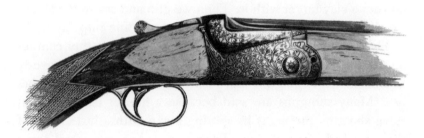

ONE AMONG
THOUSANDS

———— • 18 • ————

Our trip began on a November morning under a fine spitting rain, the kind of day that refutes any notion April is the cruelest month. Kathe, Bill, and I were driving to a farm south of Minneapolis to begin the last hunt I ever made without a dog. Two roosters sailed over the highway, narrowly missing the car. The grassy hill they landed in was not posted. This was years ago, when we weren't so fussy about the aesthetics of our hunts, so I screeched the car to a halt and we feverishly uncased guns.

One of the birds had dropped into a brushy notch near the crest of the hill. To my surprise, he was still there when I came thundering in. The rooster rose with the slow majesty of a space shuttle at the launch pad straining to overcome the claims of gravity. I almost led him by too much.

Down the hill we could see a modern farmhouse nestled in a cornfield. I knocked on the door and asked the farmer if we could hunt the slough adjoining his corn. He stared at me as if I had two heads. "You can't hunt here!" he said. "This is Bloomington! You're inside city limits!"

We retreated to the car along the highway, slinking furtively like criminals. Corporate executives commuting to their offices passed us in MGs and Triumphs. From under the snap brims of their little British driving caps, they glowered at the thugs carrying shotguns in suburbia. That was the only time in my life I regretted having a full game bag. My rooster was so huge his head dangled out one side and the great shaft of his tail stuck several feet out the other. It felt like I was packing a deer in my hunting coat.

The Bloomington Bird was the biggest rooster I've taken. His tail feathers were just over twenty-seven inches. His long spurs were glossy black with cruel ivory tips. Over the years I've thought about him often, blushing to remember how I got him.

I remembered him when I read a story by John Madson, the gifted nature writer and pheasant expert. Taking a shortcut across a marsh, Madson found himself slogging in knee-high water. Serendipitously, he walked into an island of dry ground in the middle of the slop. There he flushed and shot the grandest rooster he ever saw in a long lifetime among pheasants.

A third trophy rooster came to my attention through a fascinating story told by my old friend, Jim Layton. Jim was then managing a large wildlife area in central Iowa. A deer hunter had been on stand in some timber on the north side. He casually mentioned to Jim, "I didn't know you had turkeys here, but I saw a big one go by." Jim mulled that over. No turkeys lived anywhere nearby. But he'd already suspected there were some big pheasants back in the woods where bird hunters never went.

Jim made one special trip to bag that turkey-sized rooster. He told me, "I saw him real good, running on the ground. Steve, he's got to be the world record rooster! I could have shot him, but I wasn't going to ground-swat a bird like that. He flushed behind a tree, and that's what I shot."

The world record rooster was never seen again, though Jim later shot other timber roosters in the same area. All were superannuated trophies. He showed me a foot he took from one. The spur was about an inch long and shaped like an awl, only sharper. Woe to any rooster going up against such a weapon in a spring cockfight!

Those birds piqued my curiosity. I had always assumed that exceptionally big and attractive roosters were a random occurrence in pheasant hunting. But here were several extraordinary cocks, each living in an extraordinary place. Was there a pattern to such birds? Could a hunter deliberately set out to bag a trophy pheasant?

Of course, it isn't likely that many hunters would choose to hunt specifically for trophy pheasants. And that's just as well. There is about trophy hunting a "mine is bigger than yours" mentality that makes me wince. Trophy hunters too readily express contempt for animals that fall short of their arbitrary standards. *All* wild pheasants are wonderful game birds. All deserve the hunter's respect. Any rooster that has significance to you is a legitimate trophy, no matter what his size.

Even so, I find those rare old trophy-sized birds fascinating. There is no denying the mystique surrounding any creature that attains great size by surviving to a miraculous old age. If we understand them, we understand all pheasants better.

A trophy rooster is truly a rare bird. While pheasants have the genetic potential to live as long as ten years, none do. Pheasants die with disheartening frequency at all times of year, at all stages of their lives. The average pheasant lives seven months. Only one chick in twenty reaches its second birthday. They fall to hawks, ice storms, feral cats, collisions in flight, owls, automobiles, coyotes, blizzards, foxes, and many other causes.

Roosters mostly fall to hunters. About sixty-five percent of the fall roosters in most areas are taken by hunters. So even if the birds had no other threats, hunters would reduce a hundred roosters to four in three years.

A biologist friend calculated the odds against a rooster growing old enough to attain trophy stature. Of one hundred rooster chicks alive in spring, fifty might live until fall. Of them, only seven will make it into their second hunting season. Of them, just a single bird is likely to survive into his third season. From a mighty cohort of twenty-four thousand spring roosters, a single cock might see his sixth hunting season (and then only in the impossible case of six straight years of favorable weather).

When I was the editor of an outdoor magazine, a reader once called to report he'd shot the world record cottontail rabbit. Because even the largest rabbit lacks antlers, I was left to ponder how a trophy bunny might be scored. But for pheasants there are two common ways of defining trophy status.

Many hunters look at tail length. This is the most natural criterion in at least one sense, for it is tail length that makes lady pheasants amorous. Tail-less and bob-tailed roosters must watch in frustration as the cocks with the showiest tails service their harems in spring.

Many pheasants that go to taxidermists have tails a little over or under twenty inches long. Any bird with a tail longer than that is a striking rooster. The tail-feather contests run by some rural communities are won by feathers twenty-six to twenty-eight inches, though I've heard rumors of feathers as long as thirty-two inches.

Some hunters rate trophies by spur length. They point out that spur length is the best indicator of a rooster's age. Biologists have long used spurs to distinguish between juvenile and adult roosters. Birds with spurs longer than three-eighths of an inch are almost surely adults.

Officially, that is all you can learn from examining spurs. Yet spurs continue growing throughout life. If a rooster survives into his third or fourth year, his spurs keep changing in length and form. Some veteran hunters and a few biologists I know agree with me that extraordinarily long spurs are the hallmark of very old roosters.

Any spur over half an inch long is unusual. The only bird I sent to a taxidermist had spurs five-eighths of an inch long, though the Bloomington Bird and about a dozen other cocks I've shot wore longer spurs with nastier points. The longest spur I've heard of was collected by Jim Marti. An inch and a quarter long, it was curved like a grizzly's claw. Spurs on the oldest roosters are long, thin in profile, and wickedly sharp. Many curve upward and are black with ivory tips.

I don't regard body size as a good way to identify trophies. A plump rooster with button spurs and a scrimpy tail just doesn't seem a proper trophy. Just as many record book deer have scrawny bodies, some roosters sporting fabulous tails and spurs are senior citizens with wizened little bodies. I think a trophy should be defined by secondary sex characteristics.

Let's return to the main question. Is there a sensible way to hunt for such a rare bird as a trophy rooster? Or do big birds just come along once in a great while to anyone who slogs out enough miles in cover?

I know only one man who deliberately set out to shoot a trophy rooster. Jim Marti got the itch to win a tail-feather contest one year. "I'm not proud of that now," he told me recently, "but we were shooting so many birds that year that I got a big head and decided to win a contest."

After weeks of heavy hunting, Jim hadn't bagged a contest winner, though he had shot several grand old roosters. He thought about them. "Suddenly I realized the big birds never came from the best fields where most pheasants were," he told me. "They were off in little odd spots—you know, the kind of place you'd have to walk way the hell out of your way to get to, only you wouldn't do that because it didn't look that good in the first place."

All Marti's biggest roosters had been loners. "I'd find them in good brushy cover but not near a crop field where pheasants are supposed to be. I never found wheat or corn in their craws. They made do with the wild feed available in their lonely hideaways."

Toward season's end, Marti had a plan for bagging the contest bird. He hiked out to a secluded river bend he'd often noticed from afar without checking it out. "This spot looked okay but not great. It was just a brushy crick bottom far away from cropfields. We'd never gone there because it was so remote from everything else we hunted. You could only get to it by walking a helluva long way, and then you'd just have to turn around and walk back."

Jim's setter at the time was Ruff, a cautious worker who was so devoted to Jim she hated to be out of view of him. Ruff struck a point along the top of a steep bluff, high above the glittering prairie river. Jim waited for several agonizing moments. He had time to plan where the cock should be before he would fire.

Then the rooster began its thunderous ascent. Flushing inch by inch, a huge cock fought its way into the sky, followed by a flowing tail that seemed endless. Jim remembers, "It was like a slow motion movie. He just kept coming and coming. I thought, 'Geez, is his tail *never* going to quit?' In my mind, it seemed like he was up at my eyeball level and his tail was still down in the brush by the river. My shot dropped him in the river. He looked like a big old alligator on the water."

Jim walked home with his rooster in a bird carrier thrown over his shoulder. From time to time, the bird's tail brushed the ground.

In an effort to learn more about these rare birds, I've talked to many veteran hunters, including several biologists who hunt. Their stories of encounters with old roosters mesh with each other and with my experience. There are common patterns to these most uncommon pheasants.

Late season hunts often yield handsome cocks because the birds have had several extra weeks to develop plumage. Some of the prettiest birds I've shot were late-December Iowa roosters. Kansas outdoor writer Michael Pearce told me, "We might

get the most gorgeous roosters in the country because we shoot
through the end of January. The birds are programmed to be in
climax plumage in spring at mating time."

Although hunting late in the year will produce handsome
birds with long tails, it isn't a sure way to find those extremely
old cocks with white-tipped spurs. You need more specialized
tactics to bag a bird among thousands.

When a spring of exceptional nesting success is followed by a
mild winter, trophies become almost common. In Kansas, 1982
was a rare year of perfect nesting conditions. In 1983, Pearce
shot almost sixty second-season roosters with spurs measuring
over half an inch.

Where can trophy roosters be found? The stories of expert
hunters are surprisingly consistent on this point. Old pheasants
live in places that receive no hunting pressure.

We can only speculate why. It could be that exceptionally
wary roosters seek out forlorn little spots. Or perhaps a few
birds simply are lucky enough to locate out-of-the-way habitat
where they avoid hunters long enough to attain trophy size.
Whether trophy cocks find their solitary hideaways through
luck or innate shyness is anyone's guess. Like people, pheasants have individual personalities. Those old hermits might be
less social than most pheasants. Perhaps they march to the beat
of a different drummer.

Many giant birds come from marginal pheasant country.
Take the experience of John Cardarelli, a Pheasants Forever
employee who has hunted pheasants ardently for thirty-two
years. "Some of the nicest birds I've taken were shot in Minnesota right around my home in the northern suburbs," he told
me. "Almost nobody hunts up here. A few of these spots are
close to town limits where hunters aren't sure they can go. It
isn't great bird country, just great for trophy roosters."

I've shot some of my biggest birds north of the Twin Cities
on the extreme northern fringe of the pheasant range. Winters
there are mean. The land is marginal for row crops as well as

for pheasants. Patchy little cropfields are ringed with alder swales and marshlands as inhospitable as the moors depicted by Arthur Conan Doyle. We worked hard to find a rooster up there. But when he came, he was often a stunning bird that dwarfed the little nubbin-spurred cocks I find on public areas in prime pheasant country.

Roosters develop into trophies in refuges. Marginal pheasant country is a de facto refuge because hunters don't waste their time there. In poor pheasant country you might find islands of good habitat, and they typically harbor trophy cocks. Other refuges are created by inaccessibility. Sometimes land too difficult to walk becomes a refuge, like John Madson's marsh island.

Then there are the refuges created by hunting regulations. Rick Peifer is a University of Minnesota biologist and expert hunter who puts many miles on his English setters each fall. The largest bird he ever shot came from a refuge that had just been opened to gunning. I've written in an earlier chapter of the time four of us hunted a former refuge on Sioux land in South Dakota. We were the first hunters those roosters had seen. Our *average* bird was a taxidermy candidate.

In country with good bird numbers, you might find a trophy cock by seeking out isolated pockets of cover, as Jim Marti did. A few public hunting areas are big enough to hold cover clumps that other hunters bypass. Some of those spots lie far from all roads. Some are protected by terrain features that make getting to them difficult. The whimsical meanderings of rivers often create brushy peninsulas or islands that are difficult or uncomfortable to reach.

Trophy hideouts characteristically hold more secure cover than meets the eye when viewed from a distance. Like the hideouts of trophy whitetails, they seem quirky choices of refuge until you think about them. Trophy lairs always offer security, though they frequently are remote from the cultivated crops that are such a draw for average pheasants.

Old trophy roosters rarely come from public hunting areas. I've taken two in such places, both under special circumstances. I found my first South Dakota pheasant in a high prairie draw almost a mile from pheasant habitat. The reward for my naiveté was an old cowboy rooster with vicious spurs and a tail like a lance.

I once shot an especially large and handsome Minnesota pheasant near a willow slough in a management area just at the start of the second day of the season. I'm sure he would have slipped off to the security of private land if he'd lived another hour or two. Trophy roosters don't tolerate the pressure that ravages public lands. Yet every wildlife management area is a refuge until the moment the season starts. A hunter can get lucky there on the first day or two.

That kind of luck is more common on private land. Many farms or ranches deny access to most hunters. Some turn away all requests until late fall when the harvest has been concluded. On lightly hunted private land, you might find a trophy rooster in perfectly ordinary pheasant cover. Any time you can get on a farm not hunted by others, you stand good chances of finding the bird of a lifetime.

Several veteran hunters have confirmed my experience that trophy hideouts almost always are brushy. Grassy cover is for hens and young roosters. The big guys prefer brush, willows, alders, or even timber.

But timber is not good pheasant habitat. I've often wondered how some roosters manage to live so long in deviant habitat. Jim Layton noted the same thing, saying, "Timber simply isn't prime pheasant habitat. But a few birds manage to adapt to it. And from what I've seen, they seem to live forever."

Do trophy roosters behave differently from average ring-necks? I believe they do. And the differences are intriguing.

Though hunters talk about "smart" old roosters skulking, it is usually youngsters who sit tight and the experienced cocks who run. Early season hunting pressure teaches the surviving roosters to run instead of skulking. From that point on, pheasant hunting becomes the highly mobile sport that frustrates us so charmingly.

Thus it stands to reason that old roosters, amazing survivors that they are, would be the most elusive and hard-running sonofaguns on earth. But no. The oldest and biggest pheasants behave like juveniles. They skulk.

I can only guess why. It seems trophy roosters do not avoid hunters with their wits or their legs but by living in solitary backwaters out of the lanes of human traffic. Since these old birds never confront hunters, they do not learn the special avoidance tactics other pheasants learn to use against human predators. They have one tactic for avoiding detection: hiding quietly in their secluded refuge. They adhere to that ploy tenaciously. And then they flush.

The flush of a trophy cock is raucous and laborious. Flying seems a great effort for them. Perhaps these old birds are less vigorous than younger pheasants. Maybe they gain weight out of proportion to their wing surface area. Some of the biggest pheasants I've flushed had so much trouble getting airborne I mistook them for cripples.

I grin ruefully at the memory of one old cock I kicked up on the fringes of grouse country north of town—the same irrigation ditch Pukka and Brandy and I hunted ineptly in an earlier chapter. This bird looked as big as Pukka. He struggled so mightily to manage flight that I lowered my gun and waited for him to fall out of the sky. Even when he was thirty yards away he appeared to be mortally wounded, but gradually his flapping became stronger. I never got a shot off.

Most trophy pheasants are taken by accident. Always have been. Always will be. Ironically, many are shot by hunters who blunder into areas—like metropolitan suburbs—where smart hunters know better than to go. However it happens, shooting a trophy rooster is a rare event and special thrill. Like a record book whitetail, a trophy rooster is an uncommonly attractive and remarkable animal.

Such a bird has beaten terrible odds to have lived so long. Such a bird, should you be so fortunate as to shoot one, deserves your deepest respect. He is a bird among thousands.

SHADOWTIME
ROOSTERS

• 19 •

On Indian land several years ago, Kathe wing-tipped a rooster that darted into a cattail marsh rimmed with a tough, rubbery wall of kochia. Since the sun was just the width of a finger or two above the horizon, the world was suffused in golden light. Brandy was plunging around in the thick stuff looking for the bird when she flushed up a whitetail buck. He was a great stag the likes of which rarely exist except in the fantasies of deer hunters who have been on stand too long. The deer ran toward the sun, backlit. What I remember—and what I will always remember—was that his antlers kept striking cattail pods and making them shatter into fluff, backlit fluff, so that the deer became a dream deer moving silently in unreal light, pouring off a shower of sparks from each antler, going like a comet with a shuddering golden tail that hung in the air to show where the dream deer had passed.

I have been studying an old Kodachrome of Brandy and her master, then young and slim, with a young rooster we shot along a cut cornfield in Iowa. It is a goony photo. While the hunter grins self-consciously at his upside-down quarry, Brandy glowers like a Mafioso. Brandy purely hated the sight of a camera, knowing it meant she would have to endure at least fifteen minutes of photographic tomfoolery before she could resume hunting.

It came to me that this picture could only have been taken in November. I knew that, but didn't know how I knew. Finally I understood. It was the light. Though the noon sun shone brilliantly on that yellow field, it was the heatless low sun of November. In that flat-shooting light, each cornstalk stub cast a stubby shadow.

Pheasant hunting takes place in the time of shadows, a time of year when even midday light has a contrasty, edgy quality. In another sense, November is itself a time of shadows, the sunset of the year, the tenuous and bittersweet moment that precedes the dying of the light. As I thumb through my mental album of pheasant hunting recollections, almost all of them seem to be set in the mellow light of day's end when shadows are longest.

Few hunters seem to understand that pheasant hunting is often astonishingly productive in the last minutes of the day. That is surely one reason I have so many fond memories of shadowtime roosters. As you hunt throughout an afternoon, your shadows stretch longer and longer and often your great hopes for the day stretch thinner and thinner. Don't give up. Just as the sun goes down, pheasants often come home to roosting areas from their far-flung daytime haunts. Sometimes they walk in and sometimes they fly. If you are there, it is a memorable sight.

Jim Marti wrote me about such a moment: "1977 was the year I laid in an alfalfa field for about thirty minutes after sunset, smoking as usual, and watched pheasants flying in for the night from 360 degrees of the compass. Looked like ducks. Landed dead center in the middle of everything almost without exception. A beautiful thing in the full moon of it."

One evening Bill and I parked on a gravel road next to a plowed field that bordered a densely weeded South Dakota management area. We had six roosters that needed field dressing. In that crisp night air, pungent steam billowed out of the body cavities of the pheasants we opened. Kneeling in the ditch with a bird in my hand, I saw a weird sort of movement in the plowing. We stared. Pheasants, scores of pheasants, were returning from scattered daylight hides to sleep in the grass where they'd been born. Their legs twinkled, paused, then twinkled again as they flowed soundlessly over the broken ground. It was spooky. I was reminded of a movie I'd seen of thousands of Chinese infantrymen in leafy camouflage, sneaking en masse across a Korean battlefield. The very ground seemed to be moving.

If you are in the right place when the roosters come home to sleep the night, you'll have a flurry of action. The birds will be concentrated in small areas. Even educated cocks will be surprisingly reluctant to move when you come at them, though they might have been unapproachable all day. They have snugged in. Mark them down and go boldly for the flush. They will be there. Wherever they have touched down, they will be there. We have often shot more pheasants in the last half hour than the whole preceding day of hunting.

Yet that isn't what I remember when I cast my mind back on sunset hunts. I remember the light and the feeling of the moment, the poignant flavor of that unique and remarkable time. The day's end carries in it the image of the end of the season and the end of the year. I am always reminded that each of our lives has a natural cycle, with a beginning and an end.

One late afternoon Jerry and I walked west into a field of prairie grass that rippled in a pulsing wind like a supple living thing. Brandy and Pogo quartered ahead, backlit and outlined with sun-dazzled hair. Jerry and I walked in a trance that afternoon while the two springers performed a visual poem. For the first and last time in their lives, as each dog carved looping designs in the grass, her course was a mirror image of the other's. Brandy and Pogo seemed to have rehearsed this moment like an ice skating pair who hide their choreography in a lyric flow of motion.

For an hour Jerry and I went along that way, mesmerized. We never spoke. We didn't need to speak. It wasn't necessary to point out to each other that we were sharing an enchanted moment. And when at last Pogo flushed a rooster and I shot it, we knew the shot had crashed in on what was really going on that day—an old dog and young dog making beauty in their own special way.

I once wrote a column about how good pheasant hunting could be in the waning moments of a day. Shortly afterward, I hunted North Dakota for the first time. My late-day hunting advice earned me some friendly ribbing until I shot two roosters, each flushing when there remained but one or two minutes of legal shooting time.

One was the first rooster I took over an English setter. Jim Marti and I ambled through a grassy valley tucked between two gracefully slumping ridges. Ahead of us, Jim's companion and star stud dog, Rex, quested systematically through the cover. At last the sun drooped behind the western hills, and we turned to rejoin our friends. Neither one of us were still hunting. It was the gloaming time, when night and day walk hand in hand for a few moments.

Then Jim noticed Rex. He was locked up with an expression of dignified intensity, frozen in time and space. And in that diffuse amber light, Rex was anyone's image of a perfect dog on a perfect point in a perfect setting. It never occurred to me when I walked in that Rex might not have a bird or that it might be anything other than an old rooster of trophy stature. Indeed, that old cock had spurs like ice picks. I cut my hand on them when I picked him up, and later that night Jim cut his hand on those same rapier spurs.

The next day, Halloween Day, I rolled around on the floor of Jim's whelping barn to let a gaggle of setter pups untie my bootlaces, nip my cuffs, and chew my whiskers. One, the roguish little guy with the orange disk by his left eye, was elected to be the dog to lead me into the sunset years of my pheasant hunting career. *Hello, Spook! You and I have so much to teach each other, little buddy. I know next to nothing about pointing dogs. You know nothing of pheasants. Well, that's fine. Let the adventure begin!*

Kathe, Jerry, and I were on Sioux land in an old floodplain of the Missouri River, downstream from Pierre. At day's end we moved through knee-high wheatgrass toward some ancient prairie cottonwoods ringing an old gravel quarry. The western sun was a fat golden orb, riding low, almost touching the earth. Pogo and Brandy hit scent at the same time. Brandy worked out the line first and took off, her body tossing to and fro in that rocking horse rhythm I can still see if I shut my eyes. I trotted behind the two white springers as they romped through ribbons of wheatgrass.

Because the dogs were west of me, I saw them backlit, each white springer outlined with a dazzling halo of luminescent hair. Each galloping dog puffed plumes of light-struck steam, each backlit weedtop glowed like an incandescent filament. My mind was not on hunting. As I ran, I kept thinking, *"There's a name for the color of this light. Dammit, I know there's a name for this color! The whole world is, is—CHAMPAGNE, yes it's champagne!"*

Exactly at that instant, the rooster thrashed free of the wheatgrass and slanted toward the sun. And Jerry, bringing up the rear of the parade, saw not only the champagne grass and champagne dogs but the bird whose plumage erupted at the shot in a shower of champagne.

CODA

—— • 20 • ——

Don't try to find the pheasant fields described in this book.

Many of them are no longer there.

One of my most painful losses was the area we called Clarence's Creek, a grassy strip of land along the Missouri River. It included the creekbed where Bill shot the snake and the gully where Jerry and Kathe kicked up the largest flock of pheasants I've seen since old grinning Ike was our president. That land once belonged to you and me, purchased with our tax dollars for eternity. Then a politically messy negotiation saw control passing into the hands of the local Sioux tribe. Now someone pastures horses where we once hunted, and his neighbor plants corn right down to the river. We don't go there any more.

All too often, the land we hunted is still there, or some semblance of it. But most of the swales, marshes, brushy fences, and idle areas are gone. Gone are the hedges, soil bank forties, woodlots, terraces, and hayfields. Gone, too, are many of the sloughs, timber lines, meandering creeks, and shelterbelts.

The Rooster Factory is still there in southwestern Iowa, but its roosters are not. First to go was the huge field of soil bank weeds. When it was plowed under and put into corn, rooster production fell off. Then the farmer ran bulldozers through the big timbered draws, knocking out the cottonwoods and scalping off the multiflora tangles that held cottontails and quail coveys. He and his wife seemed genuinely to enjoy our company each fall, but we no longer come around.

I don't blame him. He means to be a survivor in the game of agriculture—a brutally competitive game with weird rules and harsh penalties for losing. Yet each time we lose another favorite pheasant field, it feels like losing a friend to cancer. We go on looking for new fields and sometimes we find them. But new fields, like new friends, never seem to fill the holes left by the ones you loved and lost.

Year by year, it becomes more difficult to get permission to hunt private land. Farms keep getting bigger and more corporate. Relations with farmers are tenser, more legalistic. Often I cannot find the person who can grant hunting permission because the man who works the land is only an employee who does not own it. Frequently, that means he lacks the emotional commitment to the land. It is a place to work, not a cherished resource to be passed on to future generations.

I am shocked by the cumulative impact on the land of decades of persistent agricultural development.

Year by year, the little bumps and hollows and odd corners of our farms have been obliterated so monster machines can motor in straight lines across monster fields. There are few sadder sights than a landscape as flat and bald as a parking lot, its topsoil whirling in clouds overhead, under which rumbles some machine not much smaller than a house.

A landscape once rich, varied, and natural has been replaced with monoculture. We need to remind ourselves that monoculture is not natural. When modern agriculture is confronted with the consequences of its ecological abuses, it typically responds by committing fresh ecological atrocities. The solutions offered for the problems of soil abuse are quick fixes involving toxic chemicals that slump inevitably into the water table.

Several recent federal programs encouraged sportsmen and conservationists because they seemed to incorporate wise land-use principles. Alas, as implemented, they have been disappointing. I see no evidence that politicians or farm policy bureaucrats have adopted a genuine commitment to sound long-range planning. Policy continues to be driven willy nilly by the winds of political expediency and market fluctuations. Our nation continues its dependency on cheap foreign petroleum. We continue to deny that the true price tag for our lifestyle is soaring national debt and the degradation of our farmland environment.

Is there reason to hope? There is always reason to hope. Several states continue to fight the holy fight with thoughtful programs that might yet improve bird numbers. The slumping farm economy motivated planners to investigate incentives for modifying farm practices to favor wildlife. Groups like Pheasants Forever have identified the most important land use issues and applied pressure for sensible changes. Pheasants now at least have an articulate voice defending their interests.

All such efforts help, and all pheasant hunters should support the folks who toil for wildlife. Their efforts reduce the rate of loss.

But there is a much bigger problem that must be addressed. There is a monster on the land called modern agriculture. It is so grievously wrong—so utterly pathological and short-sighted—that it must be radically restructured before it eliminates all our options for the future.

What is so wrong? Modern agriculture is destroying the social fabric of our food producers, frittering away precious resources of petroleum, squandering topsoil, obliterating the marshes that mitigate the drought and floods, polluting our rivers, making toxic dumps of ground water, plundering irreplaceable water resources, contributing to air pollution, eating away the ozone layer, and reducing genetic diversity in the grains we need for life.

In place of a landscape rich in variety and beauty we have erected a modern paradox: a biological desert that produces nothing except the one or two crops it is commanded to produce, and so much of them that the end product has little market value. This is agriculture by dictatorship, the sort of dictatorship that decrees: "All behavior not forbidden is compulsory." On our modern fields, all life not suppressed by some chemicals is forced to grow at unnatural rates by others.

What have we done? We have destroyed a land once vibrant and splendid in its diversity. In its place we have established the tedium and pathology of the nineteenth century factory. Inexorable economic pressures have put the land in a vise that steadily squeezes the life and color from it.

I'm not sure where we can turn for leadership for change. Our land grant universities have taught farmers that agriculture doesn't have to respect the immutable laws of biological systems. Farmers have been trained to practice the culture of food as a form of strip-mining. And even with so much refusal to acknowledge the true long-term cost of current farming styles, the whole system must be propped up with heavy infusions of tax dollars.

I have trouble seeing any winners in all this.

And the whole thing is unsustainable. Agriculture as we know it simply will not work in the future. The issue is not whether we can go on as we are but rather what radical reforms we must adopt and how much irremediable damage will be done before we implement them.

Apologists for modern agriculture tell me I should be grateful for the food factory they have created. For ridiculously little money, I can buy something that looks (but does not taste) like a carrot. Of course, I'll have to wash and scrape it to try to remove pesticide residues. Corn grown at enormous environmental expense is fed to cattle that, laced with hormones, cannot fail to bloat to marketable weights in a short time. All this so I can buy a cheap steak.

Why am I so unappreciative of this accomplishment? Why do I regret the loss of opportunity to hunt my own meat, knowing it is clean and that it led a natural life? Why do I wish someone had asked me if I wanted to forfeit the health and beauty of farmland America in exchange for cheap groceries?

Am I hopelessly romantic because I desire a return to farming arrangements now considered inefficient and old-fashioned? Obviously, I don't think so. Agriculture is now where childbirth was a few decades ago. The culmination of decades of "progress" in childbirth customs was a hospital birth in which the mother was drugged and the infant (also drugged) yanked from the womb with forceps. Be suspicious about innovations sold as progress when they seem highly unnatural.

We were talking about pheasant hunting.

Pardon me for not being more upbeat. How can I not be saddened and anguished? I have been a witness to the slow death of something I valued and loved deeply. I see that process continuing. It is easy for me to imagine solutions to the problems of modern agriculture. What is not possible is imagining *this* society finding the political will to do what it must do.

As just one consequence, we are losing the sport of pheasant hunting. Boys now grow up in a world where pheasant hunting is no longer seen as an attractive recreation. Not having known pheasants, they will not work for their future. The hunters of my generation who knew good pheasant hunting are passing from the scene. The generations in between seem ready to accept the preserve experience as a substitute for the frustrations of hunting wild pheasants in modern circumstances.

As painful as it is to observe the slow death of pheasant hunting, I mourn the passing of something larger and more important. What shocks me is the vision of the world my daughter and your son are inheriting, a world so grimly committed to economic efficiency that there is no longer room in it for bobolinks, woodpeckers, larks, cottontail rabbits, scarlet tanagers, snipe, mourning doves, raccoons, thrashers, quail, squirrels, wrens, bluebirds, muskrats, sparrows, flickers, teal, dickcissels, rails, and—yes—pheasants.

In all this, the pheasant you and I love so deeply is the canary in the mine. Although an "exotic" not originally found here, his right to a future is as absolute as that of any other species. There is nothing wrong with the pheasant that would explain his demise. What is wrong is the tyranny of a mismanaged agricultural system in which almost nothing wild is given the chance to live.

Admittedly, this is one tough canary, one that won't readily abandon his claim on his adopted land. He'll be around when Spook is but a memory, past the time when I can no longer totter about carrying a shotgun. But today there are more and more bleak wastelands where the strident yawp of the rooster pheasant is no longer heard.

Did we *mean* to do this?

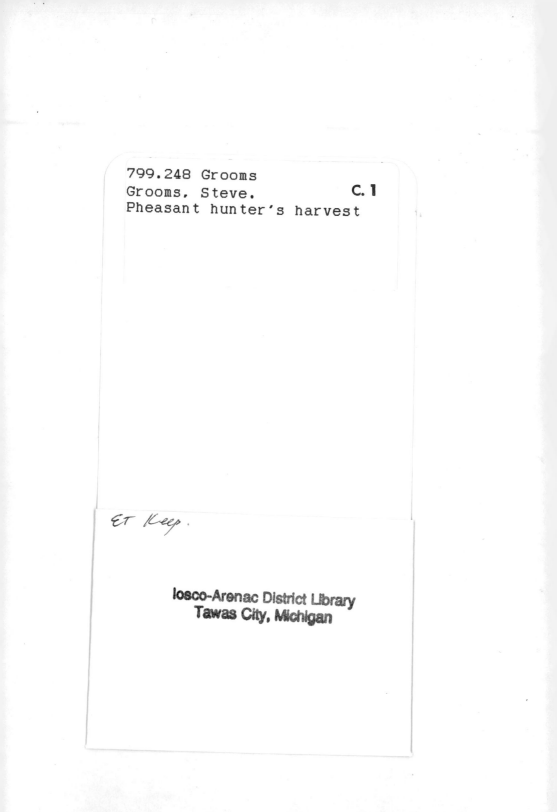